the

SPIRIT-FILLED

LIFE

ALL THE FULLNESS OF GOD

BAPTIZED | ADOPTED | TRANSFORMED | EQUIPPED | EMPOWERED | ANOINTED

THE REV. CHARLIE HOLT

EDITED BY GINNY MOONEY

Bible Study Media

The Spirit-Filled Life: All the Fullness of God

© 2015 by Charles L. Holt

Published in Lake Mary, Florida, by Bible Study Media, Inc.

Printed in the United States of America

Library of Congress Control Number: 2015949346

Hardcover Black & White ISBN: 978-1-942243-13-7
Hardcover Full Color ISBN: 978-1-942243-06-9
Paperback ISBN: 978-1-942243-14-4
Paperback Large Print ISBN: 978-1-942243-09-0
Ebook ISBN: 978-1-942243-15-1

Interior design by Lonnie G. Creative

THE SPIRIT-FILLED LIFE

CONTENTS

FOREWORD: THE RT. REV. GREGORY O. BREWER

The Christian life is a series of journeys. Some journeys are taken entirely alone, guided only by the unseen presence of Christ working in our hearts and guiding our circumstances. Other journeys are taken with others—sometimes serendipitously and sometimes intentionally. This series invites us into a short-term but intentional journey with others. And this journey is an adventure well worth taking.

By embarking on this journey, you are committing to lively conversations, Bible study, and prayer. These commitments are not haphazard; they are purposeful, for Christians believe that it is through these activities that we often discover the presence of the Holy Spirit. That is not to say that these activities are easy.

In fact, they can (and should) be deeply challenging. But if we enter into them prayerfully and intentionally, they can lead us into deep and positive personal change. The miracle is that God uses these activities to reveal His Spirit and help us, amazingly, to see where and how His Spirit is at work in us.

Fr. Charlie Holt invites us on this journey as a gentle and thoughtful guide. He is aware of the potential hazards of small group activity as well as its joys, and offers both leaders and participants clear boundaries and open-ended possibilities. I would invite you to join him and others in this adventure!

The Rt. Rev. Gregory O. Brewer, Bishop of the Episcopal Diocese of Central Florida

INTRODUCTION: ALL THE FULLNESS OF GOD

The Christian Life is a movement from Crucified to Resurrected to Spirit-Filled! Congratulations on making this journey with Jesus Christ.

With the outpouring of the Holy Spirit on the day of Pentecost, we entered into the final phase of God's plan of redemption and salvation for the world. As we explored in *The Resurrected Life* study, forty days after Jesus rose from the dead, He ascended into the heavenly realms and took the throne of heaven at the right hand of God the Father (Acts 1:1-10). Fifty days after the Resurrection, Jesus poured out the promised Holy Spirit on the Church gathered in Jerusalem and inaugurated, with all authority and power, the New Covenant between God and humanity (Acts 2:1-41).

In the letter to the Church of Ephesus, the Apostle Paul outlines the grand plan of God in Jesus Christ to redeem and restore the cosmos. Paul describes this plan as one to be put into effect "*when the times reach their fulfillment.*" The plan is pretty straightforward—to bring unity to all things in heaven and on earth under Christ (Ephesians 1:10).

The two agents actively bringing about Christ's rule on earth as it is in heaven are the Holy Spirit and us! When you and I believed in Jesus Christ as Lord and Savior of the world, we became beneficiaries and agents of the plan of redemption. You are an appointed ambassador, entrusted with the "*word of truth, the gospel of your salvation*" (Ephesians 1:13). Here is the profound promise given to those who believe:

When you believed, you were marked in him with a seal, the promised Holy Spirit, who is a deposit guaranteeing our inheritance until the redemption of those who are God's possession—to the praise of his glory. **Ephesians 1:13-14 (NIV)**

During the next six weeks of *The Spirit-Filled Life* study, you will explore how God's will for you is to baptize, adopt, transform, equip, empower, and anoint you by, with, in, and through the Holy Spirit. The six chapters are:

- *Baptized: The Outpouring of the Spirit*
- *Adopted: The Calling of the Spirit*
- *Transformed: The Fruit of the Spirit*
- *Equipped: The Gifts of the Spirit*
- *Empowered: The Work of the Spirit*
- *Anointed: The Mission of the Spirit*

I pray that as you embark on this next study in the *Christian Life Trilogy*, in your personal devotions and in community with others, God will fill you with all the fullness of His Holy Spirit. My prayer for you is joined with that of the Apostle Paul for the Church:

For this reason I bow my knees before the Father, from whom every family in heaven and on earth is named, that according to the riches of his glory he may grant you to be strengthened with power through his Spirit in your inner being, so that Christ may dwell in your hearts through faith—that you, being rooted and grounded in love, may have strength to comprehend with all the saints what is the breadth and length and height and depth, and to know the love of Christ that surpasses knowledge, that you may be filled with all the fullness of God. **Ephesians 3:14-19**

As I am faithfully yours in Him,
Charlie Holt +

WEEK ONE

BAPTIZED: THE OUTPOURING OF THE SPIRIT

When the day of Pentecost came, they were all together in one place. Suddenly a sound like the blowing of a violent wind came from heaven and filled the whole house where they were sitting. They saw what seemed to be tongues of fire that separated and came to rest on each of them. All of them were filled with the Holy Spirit and began to speak in other tongues as the Spirit enabled them.
Acts 2:1-4 (NIV)

4

DAY 1
PENTECOST SUNDAY
SETTING THE STAGE
READ ACTS 1:12-26

Have you received your gift yet?

That may sound like copy from an infomercial, but I'm actually talking about something very real and very important—the gift Jesus Christ promised His followers.

You will remember that after Jesus rose from the grave, He astonished His disciples by appearing to them over a period of forty days in various places. Then, on the fortieth day, He assembled His disciples atop the Mount of Olives and instructed them to go to Jerusalem and wait. What were they were supposed to wait for? The outpouring of the Holy Spirit!

As Jesus explained to them, *"...John baptized with water but in a few days you will be baptized with the Holy Spirit"* (Acts 1:5).

But before we talk about the Spirit's momentous arrival on the Day of Pentecost, I want to set the stage for you.

The first time we read about baptism in the New Testament is actually when Jesus was baptized by John the Baptist ("John, the Baptizer") before He began His earthly ministry. At this moment, when Jesus was talking with His disciples on the Mount of Olives,

He was assuring them that they, too, would be baptized, only with the Holy Spirit.

The disciples responded to Jesus' words with a question, *"Lord, will you at this time restore the kingdom to Israel?"* (Acts 1:6).

At first, this question seems rather "off-topic," no? In one sense, it definitely was. But in another, it was perfectly natural. Jesus had just proven Himself the Son of God by rising from the dead. The disciples were excited. Jesus was back, alive! But no sooner was He back than He was talking about going away again. They were not so excited about this. And they were confused.

If Jesus really was planning to leave again, they wanted to know one important thing first: Did He plan to reunite the kingdom of Israel before He went? Would He restore their nation to the center of world power and domination as they'd been hoping?

Jesus answered this way:

"It is not for you to know times or seasons that the Father has fixed by his own authority. But you will receive power when the Holy Spirit has come upon you, and you will be my witnesses in Jerusalem and in all Judea and Samaria, and to the end of the earth."

Acts 1:7-8

Imagine the bewilderment of the disciples! Jesus refused to tell them anything about restoring the kingdom to Israel. Instead, He uttered some mysterious words about being baptized by the Spirit. Then He promptly disappeared into the clouds. *"And when he had said these things, as they were looking on, he was lifted up, and a cloud took him out of their sight"* (Acts 1:9).

To add to the confusion, two men dressed in white appeared beside the disciples and asked, *"Men of Galilee, why do you stand looking into heaven? This Jesus, who was taken up from you into heaven, will come in the same way as you saw him go into heaven"* (Acts 1:11).

Wow. That's a lot to take in. So, what did the disciples do?

They returned to Jerusalem. Makes sense. They went back to their base, and to where Jesus had directed them to go. What did they do when they got there? *"All these with one accord were devoting themselves to prayer, together with the women and Mary the mother of Jesus, and his brothers"* (Acts 1:14).

So far, so good. The disciples obeyed Jesus by going back to Jerusalem and devoting themselves to prayer. When God calls us to wait and simply trust without knowing what's next, prayer is always a good choice.

But then, all that waiting and praying started to get old. Sound familiar? Peter—the disciple known for his impetuous spirit— wanted to *do* something, not just sit around and pray. What did Peter suggest?

Well, you will remember that the disciples were now down to eleven after the suicide of Judas. *Don't we need twelve?* thought Peter. So he convinced the others that they needed to replace Judas and fill the empty spot.

They found some good men, cast some lots, and came up with Matthias as the "replacement" disciple. Now, here's a question: When did Jesus ask the disciples to replace Judas?

He didn't.

I think the reason this story of Matthias is included in Scripture is to caution us about taking things into our own hands when the Lord's timing seems a bit slow for us. We rush ahead instead of waiting on God's guidance and provision. You see, there actually was a replacement disciple—but it wasn't Matthias.

Interestingly, we never hear of Matthias again in the Scriptures. Who do we read about instead, throughout the entire book of

Acts? Who became the famous apostle who wrote much of the rest of the New Testament? The Apostle Paul. Isn't that interesting? The disciples used a game of luck, casting lots to choose Matthias, when God had somebody waiting in the wings, soon to be called through the power of the Holy Spirit.

Sometimes we jump into a decision when the answer is soon to be presented to us. I've done that many times. Have you? We try to solve our own problems when the Lord has a solution, and if we just wait a little bit longer, we will discover it!

WHEN GOD CALLS US TO
WAIT AND SIMPLY TRUST
WITHOUT KNOWING
WHAT'S NEXT, PRAYER IS
ALWAYS A GOOD CHOICE.

REFLECT:

Are you in a place of waiting where the future seems uncertain? Why not do what the disciples first did? Devote yourself to prayer, including prayer with other believers? And then, rather than take matters into your own hands, pray for patience and wait—yes, wait—upon the Lord!

_____

_____

_____

_____

_____

_____

_____

_____

_____

_____

DAY 2
MONDAY
THE COMING OF THE SPIRIT
READ ACTS 2:1-13

When we left the disciples yesterday, they were waiting in Jerusalem for the gift Jesus had promised to send. It was a long ten-day wait!

But when the time came for the Spirit's arrival, it was truly something to behold:

When the day of Pentecost came, they were all together in one place. Suddenly a sound like the blowing of a violent wind came from heaven and filled the whole house where they were sitting. They saw what seemed to be tongues of fire that separated and came to rest on each of them. All of them were filled with the Holy Spirit and began to speak in other tongues as the Spirit enabled them.

Acts 2:1-4 (NIV)

Christians refer to the day described above as Pentecost. Pentecost means "fiftieth" (from the Greek, *pentékosté*). The Spirit's arrival on Pentecost took place fifty days after the Resurrection of Jesus. That's why Christians celebrate Pentecost fifty days after Easter, the celebration of Jesus' Resurrection.

In the Old Testament, Pentecost was a Jewish feast day celebrated fifty days after the Passover. The people of Israel would gather their first fruits for a harvest celebration. They also commemorated the giving of the Law to Moses on Mt. Sinai on this feast day.

In the New Testament, it was on the Jewish feast day of Pentecost that the Holy Spirit was first poured out with great power on the people of God, the Church. The timing of the Spirit's arrival connected the "harvest" of fruit in the Old Testament's Pentecost feast day with the "harvest" of souls that began in earnest with the Spirit's arrival on the New Testament Pentecost. Also, as the first Pentecost celebrated the Law given to Moses, the new Pentecost commemorates the Law now written on our hearts through the Holy Spirit.

So what exactly happened on the Day of Pentecost, recorded in Acts 2?

Just as Jesus promised, the disciples were baptized with the Holy Spirit. And that baptism was accompanied by an amazing display of power by God's Spirit.

First, there was a noise that's described as the sound of a violent, rushing wind. I'm not sure actual wind was blowing so much as they were hearing a sound like a rushing wind. I've heard a kind of screeching and howling here in Florida when wind whips through the branches of trees during a thunderstorm. That's what comes to mind when I imagine the sound of a violent wind.

Accompanying the sound, there was also something visual happening. The English Standard Version of the Bible describes it this way, *"And divided tongues as of fire appeared to them and rested on each one of them"* (Acts 2:3). The writer of Acts isn't describing literal fire; he is using metaphorical language to describe what is pretty much indescribable.

So the disciples *heard* something and then they *saw* something. Finally, they *did* something. They *"began to speak in other tongues as the Spirit gave them utterance"* (Acts 2:4).

Let's look a little more deeply at this event because it's one of the more interesting things that happened on the Day of Pentecost.

Now there were staying in Jerusalem God-fearing Jews from every nation under heaven. When they heard this sound, a crowd came together in bewilderment, because each one heard their own language being spoken. Utterly amazed, they asked: "Aren't all these who are speaking Galileans? Then how is it that each of us hears them in our native language? Parthians, Medes and Elamites; residents of Mesopotamia, Judea and Cappadocia, Pontus and Asia, Phrygia and Pamphylia, Egypt and the parts of Libya near Cyrene; visitors from Rome (both Jews and converts to Judaism); Cretans and Arabs—we hear them declaring the wonders of God in our own tongues!" Amazed and perplexed, they asked one another, "What does this mean?"   **Acts 2:5-12 (NIV)**

When we think of speaking in tongues, a lot of times we think of an unintelligible language, don't we? We know of people who pray in such a language as a way of communicating with God *"with groanings too deep for words"* (Romans 8:26). I have never spoken in tongues, but I am married to a person who does, and I know other people in our congregation who do.

Yet, on Pentecost, it was not unintelligible languages being spoken, but intelligible ones. And it was also a miracle of hearing. The disciples were all Galileans and yet people were hearing these men speak in their native languages.

I've heard of one other occasion where this kind of miracle took place. A seminary professor of mine, who formerly taught in Europe, told the story of being asked to speak to a conference of English-speaking students in Germany. After the conference, one of the German wait staff came up and asked the professor why he had been speaking to the English students in German.

"But I wasn't," he replied, "I was speaking English." Astounded, the server said, "But we heard everything you said in German." Hearing the professor speak about the things of the Lord in their native tongue led two of those German servers to place their faith in Jesus Christ. It was a miraculous intervention of God on behalf of souls who needed to hear God's Word in their own language. What power!

Beloved of God, as we continue in our study, we will discover that the same power of the Holy Spirit that was at work on the Day of Pentecost was also at work during that conference in Germany. And that same amazing power is available to you and me! In fact, that power is the only way we can live the Spirit-filled Life. But first we must receive the gift of the Holy Spirit. Stay tuned!

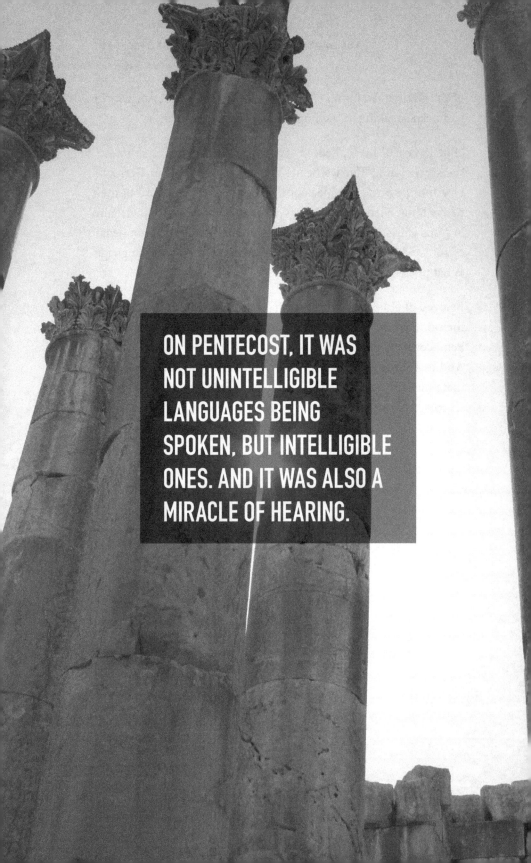

ON PENTECOST, IT WAS NOT UNINTELLIGIBLE LANGUAGES BEING SPOKEN, BUT INTELLIGIBLE ONES. AND IT WAS ALSO A MIRACLE OF HEARING.

REFLECT:

Which phenomenon of the Day of Pentecost strikes you most powerfully—the sound of rushing wind, tongues of fire, or speaking in other languages? Where have you seen the Holy Spirit move in power in your life or in the life of the Church? What was that experience like?

_____

_____

_____

_____

_____

_____

_____

_____

_____

_____

_____

_____

DAY 3
TUESDAY
THE REVERSAL OF BABEL

READ GENESIS 11:1-8

Pentecost—what a miraculous display of God's power!

Yesterday we looked at how the Holy Spirit manifested itself on the Day of Pentecost like a rushing wind and with tongues of fire resting on the disciples.

We saw how the Spirit enabled the most amazing miracle of all— the ability of the disciples to speak in other tongues, languages that those gathered in Jerusalem from various nations heard and understood as their own.

Does the story of Pentecost bring to mind another story in the Bible in which the miracle of language played a pivotal role? Perhaps you remember the Tower of Babel account in Genesis, chapter 11 of the Old Testament.

The Tower of Babel was an effort of humanity to work in collaboration to build a city with a giant tower. Their hope was that this city would keep them from being scattered upon the face of the earth. So far, so good. They were coming together as a united people with a united language for a united purpose.

The problem arose in the driving desire behind their unification: *"Then they said, 'Come, let us build ourselves a city and a tower with its top in the heavens, and let us make a name for ourselves...'"* (Genesis 11:4).

Notice the references to self: let us build *ourselves* a city and make a name for *ourselves*. There's no mention of God or His glory. Their efforts were for self-aggrandizement—making a great name for themselves.

The connection of this story to God's call of Abram (later called Abraham) in the next chapter of Genesis is very interesting. One of the things God says to Abram is, *"I will make your name great"* (Genesis 12:2, NIV). Now it's a very different thing for God to make your name great than for you personally to strive to make your name great or achieve fame. God said to Abram, *I will make you great... I will give you a great name... I will make you a great nation.* God, not Abram, would make his name great, for God's glory.

There's a joke within the Tower of Babel story. The people were coming together to build a tower that *"reaches to the heavens"* (Genesis 11:4), but the text says that the Lord had to come down to see what they were doing. That tower must not have been as high or amazing as they thought! So the Lord bent low to survey their work and their hearts, and He said, *If they keep doing this, then there's nothing they won't attempt, and it's not going to go well for them.* So He confused their language and scattered them upon the face of the earth.

Now make the comparison between the Tower of Babel and what happened on the Day of Pentecost. Who were these people who gathered in Jerusalem praising? Were they plotting together to make a name for themselves? Listen to what those who heard the disciples said: *"We hear them telling in our own tongues the mighty works of God"* (Acts 2:11).

What were they speaking about? The mighty works of God. This is a very important distinction. When we come together to make a name for ourselves, we might think, "Isn't this a good thing? Humanity's coming together to work in cooperation on something. Doesn't this please the Lord?" But if it is humanity alone making a name for itself, that's simply humanism, and God is not pleased with human efforts that exclude Him. He will confuse those efforts, divide us, and create Babel, as He did in Genesis 11—and He will do it for our own protection.

But when people come together in praise of the wonders and mighty works of God, all of a sudden the barriers of difference and the separating languages are overcome. There's a unity that takes place that is truly miraculous in nature!

Think about what happens in worship every week around the globe. People from different tongues and languages are praising God as one united voice under Heaven. And when you gather Christians from different nations and languages in a room, there's often a harmony of worship, understanding, and love like no other gathering in the world. (Visit a conference of the United Nations. That is not a united body; it's Babel!) But the Church, the assembly of God's people, is called from every tribe and nation, worshiping the Lord together as one. Only the Lord can do that!

When you see a plurality of people groups speaking one common praise to the name of the Lord Most High, that is the work of the Holy Spirit. And it began at Pentecost. The Day of Pentecost was a reversal of the Tower of Babel. Before Pentecost, you had Israel (the Jews) and then you had all the other nations, which they simply called "the Gentiles." It was either us or them. And most of our ancestors were in the "them" category of Gentiles. What Pentecost does is make possible a joining together of people of all nations and people groups in one body of Christ, tearing down racial, ethnic, and geographic barriers in amazing and miraculous ways.

That is what happened at Pentecost—a true coming together. Those who witnessed the arrival of the Spirit experienced a unity like they'd never known before. The good news is, the Holy Spirit is still with us. We are living in the age of the Spirit. That means that we, too, can experience unity as we've never known before, as Christ's one body on earth.

REFLECT:

Where have you experienced true unity in the body of Christ? In a worship service? In corporate prayer? In a small group? What was that experience like? Take a moment to pray for deeper unity in your worship community and in the Church as a whole. We can experience the miraculous oneness of Pentecost today!

_____

_____

_____

_____

_____

_____

_____

_____

_____

_____

DAY 4
WEDNESDAY
WHAT DOES IT ALL MEAN?

READ MATTHEW 9:32-34

So here's a key question: What does it all mean?

People who witnessed the events of Pentecost asked this question: *"Amazed and perplexed they asked one another, 'What does this mean?'"* (Acts 2:12, NIV).

How would you answer? Put yourself in the shoes (or sandals) of the people who were there on Pentecost, witnessing the astonishing arrival of God's Holy Spirit. How would you respond to the question: What does this mean?

Some of the people answered, *These men are crazy, they must be drunk. What a bunch of nut cases.*

Why did some witnesses respond this way? Part of the problem was their rational mindset. We've all had experiences where we've been outside our comfort zones and encountered something we've never experienced before. We simply don't have categories to explain it. It doesn't make sense. We may look to others to help us understand it or connect the dots.

A similar confusion took place at Pentecost. Some of the people saw the power of God working, and others thought they were just crazy. Why?

Sometimes, we already have our minds made up about something before it takes place. Think about it. If we've already decided that there's no God or that miracles don't take place, we will tend to interpret anything miraculous that happens as "a fluke" or "a coincidence."

When Pentecost took place, there was already a hard-heartedness present in much of the Jewish leadership. It was an entrenchment of belief that Jesus was not of God, that He was a false prophet, that He was leading people astray, or even that He was in league with the devil. In today's reading, we saw how some of the Pharisees accused Jesus of casting out demons by the power of *"the prince of demons,"* Satan (Matthew 9:34). These were just some of the things that people were saying about Jesus in the Gospel accounts. In fact, these deeply-entrenched beliefs contributed to Jesus' Crucifixion.

If you begin with a particular mindset, you will tend to interpret events according to that mindset. For the Jewish leadership who saw Jesus as a false prophet, Pentecost was just another example of those followers of Jesus doing crazy things. Digging in their heels in disbelief, they said, "They're just drunk on wine." (See Acts 2:13)

I was in the airport in Tel Aviv, Israel, during Hanukkah season. As I walked by a storefront, a man came out and asked, "Have you said your Hanukkah prayers?" I said, well, no, I hadn't, and so he ushered me into the store and put me in front of a set of candles and placed a small Jewish prayer book my hands. It was written in Hebrew. I said, "I've got to be honest with you, I'm a Christian. I can't read this. I don't know what it's saying, but I appreciate it." Suddenly, his tone completely changed, and he implored, "How can you believe in Jesus?" When I gently asked him to clarify what he meant, he said, "Well, Jesus was like a witch!"

I was completely taken aback. I didn't expect a response like that from someone who was Jewish. I imagined he might say that Jesus had been merely a prophet or a good teacher. That is what we've come to expect. But this man's perspective was that Jesus was in league with Satan and was exercising an evil form of magic. When I asked him for an example of Jesus performing dark magic, he said, "Well, he flew."

Perhaps this Jewish man was referencing Jesus' ascension into heaven. I'm not sure. But the broader point is that he had been taught by an entrenchment of disbelief to interpret anything that Jesus had done in the Gospels as evil or sorcery. The possibility that Jesus was actually demonstrating the amazing power of God— healing, loving, challenging, changing lives, and yes, ascending— wasn't even a possibility for this man. Such an explanation had been ruled out *a priori*, beforehand.

The same thing happened on Pentecost when some witnesses chose to rule out the possibility of God's power being displayed in the speaking and hearing of other languages. They believed this miracle an impossibility because of their entrenchment in disbelief. "These men must be drunk" was the only explanation they could summon.

But there were others who responded differently. *"Amazed and perplexed"* by what they had seen, these witnesses willingly opened their hearts and minds to sincerely ask the question, *"What does this mean?"* (Acts 2:12). Which kind of witness would you be?

REFLECT:

In tomorrow's devotion, we will look at how the Apostle Peter answered the question, "What does this mean?" Until then, ask yourself how you tend to respond to amazing accounts or experiences of God's power—with hard-hearted skepticism? With mockery? Or with willing belief?

_____

_____

_____

_____

_____

_____

_____

_____

_____

_____

DAY 5
THURSDAY
ON ALL PEOPLE
READ ACTS 2:14-24

Yesterday we saw that some who witnessed the events of Pentecost responded with disbelief and mockery, saying of the disciples, *"They are filled with new wine"* (Acts 2:13). But others were open to what God might be doing, a new thing in their midst. They asked, *"What does this mean?"* (Acts 2:12).

Peter became the voice of Pentecost.

Then Peter stood up with the Eleven, raised his voice and addressed the crowd: "Fellow Jews and all of you who live in Jerusalem, let me explain this to you; listen carefully to what I say. These men are not drunk as you suppose. It's only nine in the morning! No, this is what was spoken by the prophet Joel:
  'In the last days, God says,
  I will pour out my Spirit on all people.
  Your sons and daughters will prophesy,
  your young men will see visions,
  your old men will dream dreams.
  Even on my servants, both men and women,
  I will pour out my Spirit in those days,
  and they will prophesy.
  I will show wonders in the heavens above
  and signs on the earth below,

blood and fire and billows of smoke.
The sun will be turned to darkness
and the moon to blood
before the coming of the great and glorious day of the Lord.
And everyone who calls
on the name of the Lord will be saved."'   **Acts 2:14-21 (NIV)**

Let's think about Peter's explanation. He says, this is not drunkenness. It's only 9:00 in the morning. People don't get drunk at 9:00 in the morning—right?

So what is happening? Peter contends that it is the fulfillment of the promises of Scripture. What the people are witnessing had been prophesied long before as part of a grand, divine plan revealed in the scroll of the prophet Joel.

The prophecy describes several things. First, it says the Spirit will be poured out in the last days. Jesus often referred to the last days as the time beginning with His ministry. While some may think of the last days as a point in the future, Jesus and the authors of the New Testament announce that we are in the final chapter of the old heavens and the old earth. We are in the last days, which will culminate with the Second Coming of Jesus.

Granted, it's been a long period of last days; so far, over 2,000 years have passed. Yet this is exactly what was anticipated. Peter taught that the Lord's return is not slow as some count slowness. He reminds us, *"With the Lord a day is like a thousand years, and a thousand years like a day"* (2 Peter 3:8, NIV). From a divine perspective, we have only had two days!

Peter reveals that the delay, in the end, is a gracious provision from God to provide space for the people of God to repent: *"The Lord is not slow to fulfill his promise as some count slowness, but is patient toward you, not wishing that any should perish, but that all should reach repentance"* (2 Peter 3:9). We are being given the precious gift of time.

However, time is not unlimited. The final chapter of redemptive history has very specific characteristics: a universal outpouring of the Holy Spirit and a universal call to repentance.

Up until the Day of Pentecost, the Holy Spirit was only given to to particular people, such as Gideon or Samson, for particular functions. They were filled with the Holy Spirit and given unusual leadership abilities or amazing strength. Craftsmen were endowed by the Holy Spirit with skills for building the temple. The kings of Israel were called "anointed ones," meaning they were anointed by the Holy Spirit of God. Men like Moses, Aaron, David, and Elijah were considered anointed by the Spirit. Particular offices were Spirit-filled, such as prophets, priests, and kings.

But the prophecy from Joel reveals a marked change in the role of the Spirit with the advent of the last days. The Lord proclaims, *"I will pour out my Spirit on all people"* (Acts 2:17). The Holy Spirit will pour down, says Joel, on all people, even children, on sons and daughters.

My children all asked for the Holy Spirit to come into their lives when they were three or four years old. Now that amazed me— that they would want to be filled with the Holy Spirit from such a young age! But that is precisely what was prophesied—the Holy Spirit would be poured out on young and old alike. The Spirit is not just for kings and leaders; the Lord promised that even lowly servants would be filled with the Holy Spirit. *I will pour out my Spirit on all people,* says the Lord.

At the end of the Joel passage, there's a universal call to repentance. And that is preceded by a description of what will happen before the Day of the Lord: *"I will show wonders in the heaven above, signs on the earth below, blood and fire and billows of smoke"* (Acts 2:19-20).

When I was teaching middle-school students this passage, they were very interested in the signs, the blood, fire and smoke. They wanted to know, what is this about?

It's quite possible that what Joel is foretelling is the conclusion of the last days when the Lord comes back in finality. The Day of the Lord comes, and that's it. It's the moment of truth, so to speak. The key to survival on that great and awesome day is to have called upon the name of the Lord for salvation, to be filled with the Holy Spirit.

God's plan, as Peter will go on to explain, is to unite all Creation under One Head, Jesus Christ, that He might fill all-in-all with the fullness of His glorious presence. You are invited to be included in that plan by being baptized in the Holy Spirit. When you're baptized in the Holy Spirit, the Holy Spirit is poured into your heart that you might be filled with all the fullness of God. That is what really happened at Pentecost.

THE SPIRIT IS NOT JUST FOR KINGS AND LEADERS; THE LORD PROMISED THAT EVEN LOWLY SERVANTS WOULD BE FILLED WITH THE HOLY SPIRIT. *I WILL POUR OUT MY SPIRIT ON ALL PEOPLE,* SAYS THE LORD.

REFLECT:

If you had witnessed the events of Pentecost, how might you have interpreted them? Peter explained the amazing events as the Holy Spirit being poured out in the last days. Has the Holy Spirit been poured out on your heart and life? If you're not sure, ask the Lord right now to fill you with His Holy Spirit! Then watch as He works in your life, in power.

_____

_____

_____

_____

_____

_____

_____

_____

_____

_____

_____

DAY 6
FRIDAY
HOW DO WE RESPOND?
READ ACTS 2:29-41

So then we come to the next key question: How should we respond?

Following Peter's explanation of the meaning of Pentecost as the outpouring of the Holy Spirit, something interesting happens: Peter stands up and gives an impromptu sermon. He presents the Gospel message with amazing power and conviction, relating the events of Jesus' Incarnation, Crucifixion, and Resurrection, ending with these words: *"Therefore let all Israel be assured of this: God has made this Jesus, whom you crucified, both Lord and Messiah"* (Acts 2:36). Wow!

I want you to see the connection here. Any time the Holy Spirit is poured out in power, Jesus Christ is glorified. The Holy Spirit does not lift up itself—it lifts up Jesus. So Peter, filled with the Holy Spirit, did just that: he lifted up, with power, the name above all names, the name of the Lord Jesus Christ.

And how did those who were listening to this riveting message of the Gospel respond? The text says, *"When the people heard this, they were cut to the heart and said to Peter and the other apostles, 'Brothers, what shall we do?'"* (Acts 2:37, NIV).

Those who heard the words of Peter were "cut to the heart." What do you think that means? It sounds painful, doesn't it? As if a sword has pierced through our skin and bone all the way to our hearts. The word that comes to my mind is *convicted*. It's a kind of "a-ha" moment.

I've had times when I've really messed something up but been oblivious to it. Then, someone speaks a revealing word or something triggers a flood of realization and, all of a sudden, I think, "Oh no! I really blew it." I've literally felt a pain in my chest and a wave of heat flow through my body in those moments. Maybe you've experienced something similar. I believe that's what these onlookers experienced. They had just heard the truth—that they had rejected and crucified the Son of God—and they were convicted.

The writer of Hebrews describes the word of God as a sword: *"For the word of God is living and active, sharper than any two-edged sword, piercing to the division of soul and of spirit, of joints and of marrow, and discerning the thoughts and intentions of the heart"* (Hebrews 4:12).

Peter spoke the word of God to them, and it pierced their hearts. In the moment when you were convicted, what did you do next? You are faced with a choice then, either to ignore the conviction or to make a change. And if you decide to make a change, you need to know what to do next.

The people who were cut to the heart asked, *"Brothers, what should we do?"* (Acts 2:37).

Peter said to them:

Repent and be baptized every one of you in the name of Jesus Christ for the forgiveness of your sins, and you will receive the gift of the Holy Spirit. For the promise is for you and for your children and for all who are far off, everyone whom the Lord our God calls to himself.   **Acts 2:38-39**

Peter says there are two things they should do: repent and be baptized. Then God will give them two gifts: the forgiveness of sins and the indwelling of the Holy Spirit.

That first part is our part, repentance and baptism. First, what does it meant to repent? The word *repent* literally means "to turn." If I'm driving along interstate I-4 from Orlando thinking I'm heading East to Daytona Beach and suddenly see a sign saying "Tampa 50 miles," I know I'm headed the wrong way. But that realization is not enough. Unless I exit the interstate and turn my car around to drive the other direction, I won't ever reach my desired destination. Being convicted or "cut to the heart" is realizing that we are going the wrong way; repenting is actually turning around, making a change of direction.

In Hebrew, to repent is the word, שׁוּב, *shuv*, meaning "to turn away." The kids in my confirmation class love this word because it sounds like "shove." One boy said, "You've got to shove away all badness and get turned in the other direction." Yes!

In Greek, the word for repentance is μετάνοια, *metanoia*, which literally means to "change one's mind." Repentance involves a change in the direction of our thinking—a new mindset! We ask all baptismal candidates if they will renounce Satan, the corrupt powers of the world, and their own sinful desires, and turn towards Jesus as their Lord and Savior, putting their whole trust in His grace and love. Repentance is turning away from all things evil and putting one's whole trust in Jesus as our Lord and Savior. Have you done that? By changing your mindset, your heart and life will follow (see Romans 12:1-3).

What about baptism? Well, the physical act of baptism involves immersion in water. Baptism is a sacrament, an *"outward and visible sign of an inward and spiritual grace, given by Christ as sure and certain means by which we receive that grace"* (Book of Common Prayer (BCP), p. 857).

Q. What is the outward and visible sign in Baptism?

A. The outward and visible sign in Baptism is water, in which the person is baptized in the Name of the Father, and of the Son, and of the Holy Spirit.

Q. What is the inward and spiritual grace in Baptism?

A. The inward and spiritual grace in Baptism is union with Christ in his death and Resurrection, birth into God's family the Church, forgiveness of sins, and new life in the Holy Spirit. (BCP, p. 858)

Baptism is essentially a covenant between God and you. In a covenant, two parties are making agreements and bonds. When I was joined in the covenant of marriage with my wife, I made vows and she made vows. The physical sign of those vows were the gold rings we exchanged to signify our commitment and spiritual bond to one another. Something similar happens in baptism. We're making vows and promises to God; God is making promises and vows to us. We vow to turn our lives over to Jesus Christ, and He vows forgiveness and His eternal abiding presence in the Holy Spirit.

With marriage, two equals are making a mutual choice. But with God, He is the greater one who initiates and establishes the relationship with us first. We are in the subordinate, responding role. Jesus is sovereign and King over us. We are not two equals joining. This is actually great news because, in baptism, the Almighty Lord gets ahold of us forever!

The bond and covenant that God establishes in baptism cannot be dissolved. As Paul writes, *"For I am convinced that neither death, nor life, nor angels, nor rulers, nor things present, nor things to come, nor powers, nor height, nor depth, nor anything else in all creation, will be able to separate us from the love of God in Christ Jesus our Lord"* (Romans 8:38).

Once you are His, you are His forever! What astounding and wonderful news! As we exercise our faith by repenting and submitting to the sacrament of water baptism, we ask God to do His part in the covenant transaction—to grant us forgiveness of our sins (past, present, and future) and the gift of the Holy Spirit. What joy!

REFLECT:

Have you repented from every evil and given your life to Jesus Christ as your Lord and Savior? If not, do so right now! Have you been baptized in the name of the Father, the Son, and the Holy Spirit? If not, ask your pastor today about being baptized. Repentance is not a one-time action, but a patterned way of life that the Holy Spirit prompts in us. Though we can never lose our salvation—that is assured by God's promise—we can lose a sense of God's presence when we refuse to repent. So, follow the Apostle Peter's instructions: "repent and be baptized" that you might receive the forgiveness of sins and the glorious gift of the Holy Spirit.

DAY 7
SATURDAY
BAPTISM IN THE HOLY SPIRIT
READ MATTHEW 3:13-17

Yesterday we talked about the importance of repentance and baptism for followers of Jesus. We need to repent because we are sinful beings, and we are to be baptized as an outward sign of the inward reality of our new birth in Christ.

But why was Jesus baptized?

John the Baptist taught that baptism was for repentance. He prophetically challenged the people of Israel to repent of their sins and prepare their hearts for God's coming. When Jesus came to John while he was baptizing people in the Jordan River and asked to be baptized, John saw Jesus' desire for baptism as inappropriate. Jesus was the Messiah, the perfect Son of God. He did not need to repent. So why be baptized?

John would have prevented him, saying, "I need to be baptized by you, and do you come to me?" But Jesus answered him, "Let it be so now, for thus it is fitting for us to fulfill all righteousness." Then he consented. **Matthew 3:14-15**

John knew that Jesus was perfect and did not need to repent! We are the ones that need to repent. In his book, Mere Christianity, C. S. Lewis reflects on the issue:

Now repentance is no fun at all. It is something much harder than merely eating humble pie. It means unlearning all the self-conceit and self-will that we have been training ourselves into for thousands of years. It means killing part of yourself, undergoing a kind of death. In fact, it needs a good man to repent. And here comes the catch. Only a bad person needs to repent: only a good person can repent perfectly. The worse you are the more you need it and the less you can do it. The only person who could do it perfectly would be a perfect person—and he would not need it. [1]

C. S. Lewis argues that the call to repentance comes with a bitter irony: The worse you are as a person, the more you need to repent. But because of our self-centered pride, complete repentance becomes an impossible task. Those who need to can't do it fully; the One who doesn't need to is the only one who fully can.

Jesus did not need to repent; He willingly submitted to repentance and baptism to fulfill all righteousness. That means He is the only person who could truly fulfill God's call to repentance. As the only One who could truly repent, He did so on our behalf. As such, He is the only one who can lead us to that humble place.

Jesus' water baptism was just the beginning of his ministry. Later He says, *"I have a baptism to be baptized with, and how great is my distress until it is accomplished!"* (Luke 12:50). The baptism of Jesus in the river Jordan would find its completion as He stretched out His arms on the hard wood of the Cross to die for us.

So why did Jesus get baptized? Because we needed Jesus to be baptized for us. Jesus was baptized because we could not fully repent for ourselves, as we have seen. We also could not die for our own sins, which is what is required for us be born anew as forgiven beings. That is the inward reality of baptism's outward sign. Since we are not capable of doing it, Jesus does it for us.

So then, what is our baptism? Well, we are actually baptized into Jesus Christ, into His death and into His Resurrection. Baptism marks the death of the old person and the rising to new life in Christ. The Apostle Paul puts it this way:

Do you not know that all of us who have been baptized into Christ Jesus were baptized into his death? We were buried therefore with him by baptism into death, in order that, just as Christ was raised from the dead by the glory of the Father, we too might walk in new-ness of life.   **Romans 6:3-4**

This is the reason full-immersion water baptism is so powerful! As a candidate goes under the water, it is a striking visual symbol of dying and being buried (under the water), then rising up again out of the water into new life! What a beautiful picture of the way we sacramentally die and are buried with Jesus Christ, only to rise again with Him through His Resurrection.

In his book, *Anointed by the Spirit*, Bishop John W. Howe describes it this way:

> *If Jesus' baptism was a matter of his putting himself in our place, our baptism is a matter of putting ourselves in his place. We're saying that what happened to him was not only for us, but it actually belongs to us. His death was our death; his Resurrection is our Resurrection.* [2]

"His death was our death; his Resurrection is our Resurrection." What a powerful reality! In our own flesh and strength, we cannot truly repent or be baptized for ourselves. The grace and gift of God is that our repentance is complete in Christ and our baptism is a joining with Him in His baptism.

How, then, do we actively repent? We need the working of the Spirit of God in us to bring us to a place where we desire to re-pent—to turn around and go the other way. Of our own volition and prideful will, we would never turn to God. But when God puts the gentle dove of the Holy Spirit in us, He opens our hearts to new desires. By His Spirit, our wills are reoriented towards the Lord. Our blossoming faith is a gracious gift from God (See Ephesians 2:8).

We have to acknowledge paradox and mystery with respect to the intervening work of the Holy Spirit interacting with our wills. We have been granted personal responsibility to make free choices. We are called to repent and be baptized, but Jesus teaches that the wind blows where it wills: *"So it is with everyone who is born of the Spirit"* (John 3:8). God is sovereign over new birth. We are called to *"work out our salvation,"* but it is God who enables us to work and to will according to His good purposes (Philippians 2:13). We are invited to come to Jesus, but Jesus taught, *"No one can come to me unless the Father who sent me draws him"* (John 6:44).

John the Baptist taught, *"I baptize you with water, but he who is mightier than I is coming, the strap of whose sandals I am not worthy to untie. He will baptize you with the Holy Spirit and fire"* (Luke 3:16). While we call John

"the Baptist," Jesus is the true Baptizer. Jesus baptizes us with fire and the Holy Spirit. Jesus told His disciples, *"For John baptized with water, but you will be baptized with the Holy Spirit not many days from now"* (Acts 1:5).

Water baptism sacramentally points to a spiritual power that God will work as you are converted to Jesus Christ and spiritually baptized by the fire of the Holy Spirit. You must have both, water and the Spirit. The waters of baptism physically point to our immersion into our new life in the Spirit. However, it is possible to have been water baptized without Spirit baptism. Without the baptism of the Holy Spirit, water baptism is just water.

Like John, we are called to faithfully water baptize those who come to us in faith and repentance. But, Jesus is the one who baptizes with the Holy Spirit, and that baptism is out of our control and timing! Mysteriously, our faithful actions and the Spirit's will are connected.

Baptism is just the beginning of your Christian life. The fire kindled by the Spirit in your baptism burns for your entire life, for all eternity. None of us are experts on the Spirit-filled life. But what does it mean to walk in the newness of life? It's a tremendous question. Repenting is about dying to self that we might be raised in the new life of Christ. But that is just the beginning! It remains for us to walk in the Spirit of the living God. If you have never experienced the indwelling power of spiritual baptism, ask the Lord to baptize you in the Holy Spirit. He promises to give the Holy Spirit to those who ask (Luke 11:13).

REFLECT:

Come to the waters. Come and receive the Holy Spirit. Jesus the Baptizer would set you on fire to live for Him! May the Holy Spirit be poured out on you like the dove from heaven. May your heart be converted in Christ as the baptism of the Spirit's presence manifests in your life. Ask for this gift of God and receive the Holy Spirit's passion!

_____

_____

_____

_____

_____

_____

_____

_____

_____

_____

ADOPTED: THE CALLING OF THE SPIRIT

But when the fullness of time had come, God sent forth his Son, born of woman, born under the law, to redeem those who were under the law, so that we might receive adoption as sons. And because you are sons, God has sent the Spirit of his Son into our hearts, crying, "Abba! Father!" So you are no longer a slave, but a son, and if a son, then an heir through God.

Galatians 4:4-7

DAY 8
SUNDAY
A SPIRIT OF ADOPTION

READ ROMANS 8:12-17

I remember the day my father and stepmother announced they were adopting a baby girl. I was 16. In an instant, I received my second sister, Becky.

Becky has been a tremendous blessing to our family. A few years back, I had the privilege of serving Becky and her new husband as the celebrant at their wedding. I marveled at how the Lord has matured my young sister into a beautiful woman inside and out.

In addition to Becky, I have two sisters-in-law who were adopted. So, between my wife, Brooke, and me, we have three adopted siblings. From our family's perspective, there is no distinction between the members who joined our family through adoption and those who were born into it. Each child is embraced as a treasured gift and blessing from the Lord.

For those of us who have experienced adoption personally, it's easy to understand how rich a metaphor God is using when He calls us adopted children of God. John writes, *"See what kind of love the Father has given to us, that we should be called children of God; and so we are"* (1 John 3:1). And the Apostle Paul says to the Church at Ephesus, *"In love [God] predestined us for adoption as sons through Jesus Christ, according to the purpose of his will..."* (Ephesians 1:4-5).

If you are a Christian, then you are adopted into the family of God as brothers and sisters with Jesus Christ. The Apostle Paul writes in his letter to the Romans, *"[But] you have received the Spirit of adoption as sons, by whom we cry, 'Abba! Father!' The Spirit himself bears witness with our spirit that we are children of God, and if children, then heirs—heirs of God and fellow heirs with Christ..."* (Romans 8:15-17).

Abba is a child's name for "Father," but one that implies great warmth and intimacy, like "Daddy." My daughter, Ashton, called me Abba when she was first learning how to talk. I was her Abba. "Mama, Dada, Abba"— these are the first words that children form and associate with the most significant objects of their affection and trust: their parents.

The same is true of our relationship with God. As children of God, we look to Him as the primary object of our affection and our trust. He is our Abba, our Father.

Do you have that childlike affection for God in your life? Do you find yourself calling out to Him as your Father, your Abba? Do you seek His affirmation with cries from your heart in the midst of the struggles and challenges of this life? Paul is saying that these very prayers in which we cry, "Abba! Father!" testify, along with God's Spirit, that we are indeed children of God. Your reliance on God as your Father for provision, protection, and direction should reassure your heart that you are indeed a true child of God.

Consider the implications of this relationship with God as your Father—wonderful implications!

First, you are actually a brother or sister to Jesus. God brings you into His family and gives you an equal standing with His Son,

Jesus, as your brother. And as a brother or sister of Jesus, you are actually an heir, a co-heir with Him, of the Kingdom of God. When you have the Spirit of adoption, you are a co-inheritor with Jesus Christ of His kingdom, His rights, and His privileges. They are granted to you. What He receives, you receive! How amazing.

And this inheritance can never be taken away. It is sealed by the Holy Spirit. And the Holy Spirit, also called the Spirit of adoption, testifies along with your spirit that you are, indeed, a beloved and treasured child of the Most High God. What a privilege!

REFLECT:

Do you have any personal experience with adoption? How does this experience help you better understand your status as God's adopted child? If you aren't sure if you are a child of God today, cry out to him, "Abba, Father!" and ask Him to bring you into His family. His loving arms will welcome you and never let you go!

_____

_____

_____

_____

_____

_____

_____

_____

_____

_____

_____

DAY 9
MONDAY
IS THE HOLY SPIRIT IN YOU?
READ ROMANS 8:9-11

One of the most prevalent false teachings in the world today—taught even by some well-meaning, but misguided, teachers in the Church—is that there are multiple paths to God.

I have heard it put this way: There is a vast mountain with many roads that all lead to the pinnacle at the top, where God is.

Jesus taught something quite different. He said there are only two roads, or paths, in this world. One is broad and easy and leads to destruction; the other is narrow and difficult, but leads to life.

Enter by the narrow gate. For the gate is wide and the way is easy that leads to destruction, and those who enter by it are many. For the gate is narrow and the way is hard that leads to life, and those who find it are few.   **Matthew 7:13-14**

Jesus is the gate and the narrow way. He says of Himself, *"I am the gate; whoever enters through me will be saved"* (John 10:9, NIV). And in another well-known verse, Jesus says, *"I am the way, and the truth, and the life. No one comes to the Father except through me"* (John 14:6).

Jesus is the only way to the Father. The Word clearly teaches that the path to God the Father is through God the Son. For by faith, *"we have peace with God through our Lord Jesus Christ. Through him we have also obtained access by faith into this grace in which we stand"* (Romans 5:1-2). Jesus is the exclusive and unique way to God the Father.

But is there an exclusive and unique path to God the Son?

Jesus is the only way to the Father; but there is also only one way for the work of Jesus to be applied to our lives—through the person and work of the Holy Spirit, also called the Spirit of Christ.

You, however, are not in the flesh but in the Spirit, if in fact the Spirit of God dwells in you. Anyone who does not have the Spirit of Christ does not belong to him.   **Romans 8:9**

The historic events of Jesus' death on the Cross and Resurrection cannot help you personally until they are activated in your life. That happens only by the person and work of the Holy Spirit. If the Holy Spirit is not in you, then you are still alienated from God, dead in your sins, and under the dark cloud of the law of condemnation.

There is a drink commercial that asks, "Is it in you?" This is a critical question for us, too. That's because the key that unlocks the power of Christ's death and Resurrection for the individual believer is the Holy Spirit. It's the linchpin. It's the activator. The Holy Spirit turns on the ignition. It is the spark plug that ignites the engine. It's the living yeast that makes the dough rise. It's what makes it all work.

The Apostle Paul puts it this way:

If Christ is in you, though the body is dead because of sin, yet the spirit is alive because of righteousness. But if the Spirit of Him who raised Jesus from the dead dwells in you, He who raised Christ Jesus from the dead will also give life to your mortal bodies through His Spirit who dwells in you.   **Romans 8:10-11, NASB**

So the application of the work of the Son, Jesus, both to forgive sins and to conquer death, comes to us through the gateway of the Holy Spirit.

One may think of the narrow path in this way:

US → HOLY SPIRIT → JESUS, THE SON → THE FATHER

The only way we can have access to the Father is through the Son who has reconciled us and given us direct access to a restored relationship with the Father. Engagement with the Son comes through the person and work of the Holy Spirit. The Holy Spirit is the Spirit of Christ who is given to us that we might be united and adopted into the family of God.

For all who are led by the Spirit of God are sons of God.
                                                  Romans 8:14

The Father reveals Himself through the Son, and the Son reveals Himself through the outpouring of the Holy Spirit. The point of the Scriptures is that you cannot have God unless you have a relationship with God in all three persons of the Trinity: Father, Son, and Holy Spirit. To remain separated from one person of the Trinity of God is to remain separated from God. To know God is to know the three persons of the Trinity and the fellowship of love that is shared between the three-in-one.

So apart from the Holy Spirit, the Cross and Resurrection of Jesus Christ remain external and foreign realities. But when they are activated in your life by the Holy Spirit, they become forgiveness from sin and life everlasting!

REFLECT:

Is the Holy Spirit in you? What evidence of the Spirit's work do you see? If you are not sure that you have the Holy Spirit, pray now: "Father, send your Holy Spirit to dwell in me that I may be adopted into your family and sealed forever as Your own. Amen."

_____

_____

_____

_____

_____

_____

_____

_____

_____

_____

DAY 10
TUESDAY
THE FATHER'S GOOD GIFTS
FOR HIS CHILDREN
READ LUKE 11:9-13

Yesterday, we wrestled with the question: "Is the Holy Spirit in you?"

If you feel that the dynamic of the Spirit's work drawing you through the Son to the Father is not taking place in your life, then it should give you cause to turn and reach out to the Lord in prayer. So often we do not have in our lives because we have not asked.

Ask, and it will be given to you; seek, and you will find; knock, and it will be opened to you. For everyone who asks receives, and the one who seeks finds, and to the one who knocks it will be opened.
Matthew 7:7-8

There can be some fear and trepidation in asking God for His Holy Spirit. But the Apostle Paul encourages us that we are not recipients of the spirit of slavery (to sin) that would lead us back into fear, but rather recipients of the *"Spirit of adoption as sons, by whom we cry, 'Abba, Father!'"* (Romans 8:15).

God does not desire to relate to us from a posture of scaring us into submission to His will or threatening us to conform "or else!" He is not ruling over us like Zeus in a storm cloud with lightning bolts in his hands ready to hurl our way on an angry whim.

Rather, God wants to give us good things. In fact, Jesus specifically encourages us to ask the Father for the Holy Spirit. He compares our Heavenly Father to earthly fathers who, though sinful, know how to give good gifts to their children:

What father among you, if his son asks for a fish, will instead of a fish give him a serpent; or if he asks for an egg, will give him a scorpion? If you then, who are evil, know how to give good gifts to your children, how much more will the heavenly Father give the Holy Spirit to those who ask him!   **Luke 11:11-13**

If you have (or had) a good relationship with your earthly father, then you can instantly recognize the truth of Jesus' analogy. If your earthly father was generous with you, then you understand the desire of the Father to be abundant in His gifts and love for you.

However, for some people, there is a spiritual barrier to relating to God as "Father" because their relationship with their earthly father was difficult. In these cases, the whole image of fatherhood can be distorted, particularly if there was emotional or physical abuse. A person may not see that God the Father truly does have good things for His children.

I went through a season in my college days when my relationship with my earthy father was tense and strained. Interestingly, that was the very time when I began my personal relationship with God.

My immature perception of God was that He was always angry with me, just waiting for me to mess up so that He could lower the boom or give stern correction. One day, a college friend named Jill challenged me: "You have taken your relationship with your earthy father and imposed it on God." She continued, "God the Father is not like your earthy father." Her words hit me like a ton of bricks—Jill was right!

My strained relationship with my earthly father had caused me to misunderstand God the Father. In her gentle but truthful confrontation, my friend liberated me to see God the Father in a completely new way, as a generous and loving Father who desired to be in relationship with me. I did not know Him, or understand His lovingkindness toward me. But with a word, I was now liberated from my false view of God to learn the true nature of the Father's heart!

Here is the wonderful byproduct: as my relationship with my Heavenly Father strengthened and became more true and healthy, so did my relationship with my earthy father.

As I have grown older and had children of my own, I have appreciated the difficulties of being a human father. It is not easy to get through to your children that you love them and care about them. I now see that some of the "gifts" I wanted from my earthly father were denied to me not because he was hard or uncaring, but precisely because he did love me. He cared enough to see me grow up to become a strong person.

Jesus appeals to our love and care for our own children. He knows that we want what is best for them, even though we are sinful and imperfect in our love. If you are a parent, tap into that instinct to desire good things for your children. Recognize that it is not just a God-given gift, but also a reflection of God's own parental love for us!

God the Father desires to give good gifts to His children—that means you and me. Ask, seek, knock. The Heavenly Father will give the best gift, the Holy Spirit, to those who ask Him!

REFLECT:

How has your relationship with your earthly father affected your view of God the Father? Have you imposed your earthly father's shortcomings on God? Why not ask God to help you see Him as the generous, loving Heavenly Father that He is. And ask Him for His Holy Spirit!

_____

_____

_____

_____

_____

_____

_____

_____

_____

_____

DAY 11
WEDNESDAY
FROM FEAR TO FREEDOM, SLAVE TO SON

READ ROMANS 7:7-25

Today, let's think about why we need to be adopted.

What do the Scriptures reveal to us about our standing with God and the nature of our condition prior to adoption into the family of God?

In his magnificent letter to the Romans, the Apostle Paul reveals that, prior to our adoption into the family of God, we are in a state of slavery and bondage to a sinful human nature what he describes as the dominion of death (Romans 6:9). Paul identifies three controlling forces or laws that affect us: the Law of God, the Law of Sin, and the Law of the Spirit.

First, the Law of God was given to Moses as an external set of commandments. We often call it the Torah, the first five books of the Bible. It is sometimes referred to as the Law of Moses or the Law of God. For Paul, it's just simply "the law."

For I would not have known what it is to covet if the law had not said, "You shall not covet." But sin, seizing an opportunity through the commandment, produced in me all kinds of covetousness. For apart from the law, sin lies dead. I was once alive apart from the law, but when the commandment came, sin came alive and I died. The very commandment that promised life proved to be death to me. For sin, seizing an opportunity through the commandment, deceived me and through it killed me. So the law is holy, and the commandment is holy and righteous and good. **Romans 7:7-12**

Paul is using the example of one of the Ten Commandments: *"And you shall not covet your neighbor's wife. And you shall not desire your neighbor's house, his field, or his male servant, or his female servant, his ox, or his donkey, or anything that is your neighbor's"* (Deuteronomy 5:21, cf. Exodus 20:17).

In our day "Do not covet" means not to desire your neighbor's spouse, cars, house, profession, or life. Back in the day, sheep and cattle were the source of pride and abundance. Then, as now, whether sheep or cars, it was about comparing our lives to others and "keeping up with the Joneses."

For Paul, coveting was a very real internal struggle. He was an unmarried, celibate man and a missionary itinerant. He owned no home and had very few possessions. In his letters, we read that all he owned was a cloak, a staff, and some scrolls—not much. When Paul went into the prosperous cities of Corinth or Athens, housed in others' homes, would he desire the blessings they had? Perhaps he thought to himself, "I want this wife and family, this home, this life." By his own admission, Paul struggled with coveting.

Yet the law against coveting, like all of God's laws, is a good rule. If we followed it perfectly, it would mean contentment and more harmonious relationships. Unfortunately, the Law of God does not lead to that result.

Why? Because of the dynamic of the second law Paul describes, the Law of Sin.

So I find it to be a law that when I want to do right, evil lies close at hand. For I delight in the law of God, in my inner being, but I see in my members another law waging war against the law of my mind and making me captive to the law of sin that dwells in my members.

Romans 7:21-23

Paul is a divided person; there is a battle within. He is fighting between following the Law of God and succumbing to the Law of Sin—the evil that lies close at hand. And, as he writes, our "flesh" is a captive to this Law of Sin.

For we know that the law is spiritual, but I am of the flesh, sold under sin. For I do not understand my own actions. For I do not do what I want, but I do the very thing I hate. Now if I do what I do not want, I agree with the law, that it is good. So now it is no longer I who do it, but sin that dwells within me. For I know that nothing good dwells in me, that is, in my flesh.   **Romans 7:14-18**

One of the great philosophical debates is whether humans have "free will." Certainly we all have freedom to make choices and receive the blessing or consequences of those choices. Yet, what Paul is describ-

ing is a pervasive bondage of our will to the sin nature—a state of slavery. His choices are being governed in such a way that he is going where he does not desire to go, as if by the force of a tyrant, keeping him from choosing the way that his mind knows is right and is pleasing to God.

For I have the desire to do what is right, but not the ability to carry it out. For I do not do the good I want, but the evil I do not want is what I keep on doing. Now if I do what I do not want, it is no longer I who do it, but sin that dwells within me.   **Romans 7:18-20**

Sin is holding him captive—his will is not free.

Here is the fundamental problem for anybody who's trying to live a holy life: The sin nature cannot be overcome by a rule or by laws. Trying to follow the Law of God on our own only leads to bondage to the Law of Sin and Death. This is why Paul cries out for a savior:

Wretched man that I am! Who will deliver me from this body of death? Thanks be to God through Jesus Christ our Lord! **Romans 7:24-25a**

If we're going to be saved from death, we're going to need something that will overcome the Law of Sin, that bondage to the sin nature. We need the third law—the Law of the Spirit!

REFLECT:

When have you experienced a "battle within," knowing the right thing to do but being unable to do it? In what way did your situation feel like "slavery" or "bondage?" Have you ever been "set free" from a particular sin by the power of the Spirit? Do you desire to? Take it to God now.

_____

_____

_____

_____

_____

_____

_____

_____

_____

_____

DAY 12
THURSDAY
THE LAW OF THE SPIRIT OF LIFE
READ ROMANS 8:1-8

We first encounter the language of "sonship" in the Old Testament when the Lord redeems Israel from its bondage to slavery in Egypt:

"When Israel was a child, I loved him, and out of Egypt I called my son."   **Hosea 11:1**

The Gospel writer Matthew sees this verse not only as a description of God's redemption of Israel, but also as a prophecy fulfilled when Joseph took Mary and the infant Jesus to Egypt to escape Herod's threats: *"This was to fulfill what the Lord had spoken by the prophet, 'Out of Egypt I called my son'"* (Matthew 2:15).

The imagery of sonship extends beyond Israel and Jesus to us and our inclusion as adopted children of God. The aim of the New Covenant in Christ' blood is to liberate many sons and daughters of God from a more sinister and universal bondage than that of the Egyptian pharaoh—the cruel bondage of our sinful human nature.

Yesterday we considered the internal struggle of our wills to the flesh nature and the inadequacy and danger of the external Law of God. The Law of Sin and the Law of God result in a seemingly hopeless interaction that Paul calls the Law of Sin and Death. These two forces in our lives—sin and death—are enslaving and deadly. Yet God has resolved both of these for us in Jesus Christ through the Spirit of adoption.

Paul announces:

There is therefore now no condemnation for those who are in Christ Jesus. For the law of the Spirit of life has set you free in Christ Jesus from the law of sin and death.   **Romans 8:1-2**

The Law of God is powerless to control the sin nature. All it serves to do is bring fear, guilt, and condemnation—not because the Law is bad, but because we can never fully follow it. But God Himself devised a solution:

For God has done what the law, weakened by the flesh, could not do. By sending his own Son in the likeness of sinful flesh and for sin, he condemned sin in the flesh, in order that the righteous requirement of the law might be fulfilled in us, who walk not according to the flesh but according to the Spirit.   **Romans 8:3-4**

We could not find a more clear statement of why religious rules and regulations are inadequate to bring salvation. External laws are powerless over the internal sinful flesh! The need is for an internal force that will literally "put to death" the power of evil within the human heart. That internal force is the Holy Spirit of God.

I remember when I first understood my need to be filled with God's power in order to overcome sin. I was living in a fraternity house at the University of Florida and struggling with a way of life I knew to be wrong. I remember reading Romans chapter 7 and resonating with Paul's struggle against his own sin nature: *"For I have the desire to do what is right, but not the ability to carry it out. For I do not do the good I want, but the evil I do not want is what I keep on doing"* (Romans 7:18-19). How true those words were for me. But what was the solution?

Then I read the next chapter, Romans 8, and it liberated me! I had been trying to please God by pulling myself up by my own boot-straps—and failing miserably at that. I read the words, *"There is therefore now no condemnation for those who are in Christ Jesus. For the law of the Spirit of life has set you free in Christ Jesus from the law of sin and death"* (Romans 8:1-2). At that very moment I prayed to God, "Father, fill me with your Holy Spirit!" That is when the Lord activated my heart to want and desire the aims of the Father.

Like so many others, I was trying to live with my mind set on the flesh and still follow God (or not!). But when I realized that I was a deeply loved child of God and free from the condemnation of the external laws... Wow! I suddenly became very peaceful and trusting of the internal Spirit of God working within me. The Lord gave me a new mindset and a heart reset.

For those who live according to the flesh set their minds on the things of the flesh, but those who live according to the Spirit set their minds on the things of the Spirit. For to set the mind on the flesh is death, but to set the mind on the Spirit is life and peace. For the mind that is set on the flesh is hostile to God, for it does not submit to God's law; indeed, it cannot. Those who are in the flesh cannot please God.   **Romans 8:5-8**

Just as the Israelites had to learn a new way of thinking about themselves, so do we. We must no longer have a slave mentality of dependency on the flesh nature. We are free from it! But we must orient our minds and hearts to the law of the Spirit of Life. God is calling us out of Egypt into freedom.

REFLECT:

Do you see yourself as a child of God? How does this affect your life? God wants to change you from the inside out through the Spirit of adoption. Today, make a decision to set your mind on Him and His liberating Spirit. He loves you and is leading you from death to life, from fear to freedom!

_____

_____

_____

_____

_____

_____

_____

_____

_____

_____

_____

DAY 13
FRIDAY
THE ADOPTION PROCESS
READ EPHESIANS 1:3-14

Parents of foster or adoptive children will tell you this again and again: Adoption is a process.

The first phase is simply the decision to adopt. Unlike the natural birth process, adoption involves a clear, conscious choice on the part of the parents to bring a new child into their lives. Once a child is identified and chosen, the parents are in for an arduous and challenging gauntlet of paperwork, interviews, research, travel, and financial and emotional expense. What gives adoptive parents the endurance to get through this phase is the sheer love they have for the child and the determination to secure that child against all odds and over any barriers.

We must never forget that the Lord has done the same for us! He knew us before we knew Him:

Blessed be the God and Father of our Lord Jesus Christ, who has blessed us in Christ with every spiritual blessing in the heavenly places, even as he chose us in him before the foundation of the world, that we should be holy and blameless before him. In love he predestined us for adoption as sons through Jesus Christ, according to the purpose of his will, to the praise of his glorious grace, with which he has blessed us in the Beloved. **Ephesians 1:3-6**

The process of our adoption into the family of God began long ago—before the foundations of the world were laid. The Father has loved you and me from before time and forever. Understanding God's pre-determination to secure us as His children before we were even born can bring a great sense of self-worth and value.

Once a little girl was playing on the playground with other children. When they began teasing her about being adopted, she responded, "My parents chose me; your parents got stuck with you!" Indeed. You are special because God chose you as His child. He called you to Himself, adopted you, and you are His.

Once a child is brought into a family, there is often a honeymoon phase during which the child and parents enthusiastically embrace their new relationship. Parents receive the adoption papers that confirm the child belongs to them with all of the appropriate legal seals. There is a great celebration when the child is brought home. The child is a full member of the family now. That moment of realization can be euphoric! It also can bring some fear and trepidation as a new reality is born.

There are similarities to our adoption by the Lord:

In him you also, when you heard the word of truth, the gospel of your salvation, and believed in him, were sealed with the promised Holy Spirit, who is the guarantee of our inheritance until we acquire possession of it, to the praise of his glory. **Ephesians 1:13-14**

You may remember the day when you first heard the word of truth, the Gospel of your salvation. How did you receive the news of your adoption into the family of God?

In the verse above, Paul explains that we have the full rights of inheritance as adopted children of God. Your adoption papers are signed and sealed! Your inheritance of eternal life is secure. The guarantee is the Holy Spirit of God.

The challenge of your adoption process now becomes living into that new reality.

Parents who have adopted children, particularly of an older age, will tell you that there are significant challenges to raising children who are not yours by natural birth. There is no way to know the extent of the emotional and physical trauma the children may have experienced thus far in their lives. There also may be genetic dispositions that are completely unknown to the new parents that manifest later in life.

There is also the issue of bonding. In biological birth, bonding occurs from the womb. But in adoption, it takes time—lots of time—for love and security to grow between the child and the parents. The parents must constantly reaffirm their unconditional love to the child, sometimes to a child who is not acting very lovable. The child must learn to trust the parents' love before developing a lasting bond with them.

I love the words of Jen Hatmaker as she reflects on the lessons she has learned about God's love as an adoptive parent fighting for her children's love and growth:

> *Anything worth fighting for is worth fighting through, and adoption is one of them. I can hardly think of something closer to God's character, who is the "Father to the fatherless, defender of widows — this is God, whose dwelling is holy." Certainly, we are his difficult children who spaz out and pull away and manipulate and struggle. We distrust His good love and sabotage our blessings, imagining our shame disqualifies us or that God couldn't possibly be faithful to such orphans. But He is. We are loved with an everlasting love, and it is enough to overwhelm our own fear and shame and humanity.* [1]

The Father has called you into His family, yet the challenge to know and trust His love is real. This is why He has placed His Spirit

GOD CHOSE YOU AS HIS CHILD. HE CALLED YOU TO HIMSELF, ADOPTED YOU, AND YOU ARE HIS.

in our hearts, as a witness to us that we are His. You came to the family with lots of challenges, struggles, and natural dispositions, as did I. The Father would have us know His love for us:

...that you, being rooted and grounded in love, may have strength to comprehend with all the saints what is the breadth and length and height and depth, and to know the love of Christ that surpasses knowledge, that you may be filled with all the fullness of God.

Ephesians 3:17-19

REFLECT:

Do you ever struggle with believing that God truly loves you? What is behind that struggle? Today, remind yourself that the God of the universe chose you to be His child before the earth began. Call out to the Holy Spirit to reassure your heart of your adoption and eternal inheritance in His Kingdom. The Holy Spirit is your seal of adoption.

_____

_____

_____

_____

_____

_____

_____

_____

_____

_____

DAY 14
SATURDAY
SECURITY AND ASSURANCE
READ ROMANS 8:18-30

The eighth chapter of Paul's letter to the Romans begins and ends with wonderful promises: *There is no condemnation for those in Christ Jesus* (Romans 8:1), and *Nothing can separate us from the love of God* (Romans 8:38-39).

The entire chapter is about our adoption and standing as God's children.

But what assurances can we have that we are indeed adopted children of God?

One way we can know is that we experience a constant struggle to live into our sonship and not be drawn back into the old ways of slavery.

For all who are led by the Spirit of God are sons of God. For you did not receive the spirit of slavery to fall back into fear, but you have received the Spirit of adoption as sons, by whom we cry, "Abba! Father!" The Spirit himself bears witness with our spirit that we are children of God...   **Romans 8:14-16**

We all struggle and suffer in this fallen world against sin, temptation, and evil. And that suffering may cause us to doubt God's love for us or our legitimacy as God's children. Yet the very fact that we are struggling is a testimony that we are legitimately His! If we were still in the flesh, we would have no conflict or struggle. Our very cries to God as "Father" let us know that we are indeed His children. It is God's Spirit that prompts us to cry out to Him as our Father when we are in need.

As we do, God the Father is constantly reassuring us by the inward Spirit of adoption that we are His so that we will not fall back again into a spirit of slavery, governed by fear.

What is the Spirit of adoption? It is the Holy Spirit, the Spirit of sonship that comes from Jesus Christ. By putting His Spirit within us, Jesus has given us the same relationship that He has with His Heavenly Father. We are brothers and sisters of Jesus Christ and co-heirs with Him as children of God.

The larger plan of God is that, through the outpouring of the Holy Spirit, the Father is calling many children to Himself. Paul describes the whole creation as groaning as in the pains of child-birth as it awaits the revealing of these sons and daughters of God. Like childbirth, the suffering and pains are temporary and not worth comparing to the glorious revelation of those children (Romans 8:18-25).

Because we are all still in the difficult process of fully living into our own adoptions as well as awaiting the full inclusion of all the Father's adopted children, we groan and long for that moment:

For we know that the whole creation has been groaning together in the pains of childbirth until now. And not only the creation, but we ourselves, who have the firstfruits of the Spirit, groan inwardly as we wait eagerly for adoption as sons, the redemption of our bodies.
Romans 8:22-23

The Lord would give us even more assurance of our inclusion in the family of God as the Holy Spirit *"helps us in our weakness"* and ministers to our hearts with *"groanings too deep for words"* (Romans 8:26). In this time of suffering, longing, groaning, and challenge, the Holy Spirit serves as a communication mediator between us and the Father, that we might know His will and love for us and that He might hear our hearts' cries.

In the midst of this earthly struggle, Paul assures us, we can know that *"for those who love God all things work together for good, for those who are called according to his purpose"* (Romans 8:28). Because we have been adopted and chosen by God, He who initiated our relationship with Him will also bring it to a glorious completion.

For those whom he foreknew he also predestined to be conformed to the image of his Son, in order that he might be the firstborn among many brothers. And those whom he predestined he also called, and those whom he called he also justified, and those whom he justified he also glorified.   **Romans 8:29-30**

Notice that there is no loss or slippage in this process of bringing the Father's children to the full glory of salvation. He does not say "some of those," but rather those foreknown, predestined, called, and justified will also be glorified! What the Father begins, He will bring to completion. This is why Paul can assert with absolute confidence at the end of Romans 8 that there is nothing that can separate us from the love of God in Christ Jesus our Lord—nothing!

As a child of God, He has got you. You are His; His love for you is secure and eternal.

REFLECT:

What temptations, fears, or suffering have caused you to doubt that you are a child of God? What reassures your heart that you are indeed His? There is power in speaking the truth aloud. Right now, say out loud, "I am a loved, chosen, and adopted child of God. Nothing can separate me from His love—nothing. I am His forever!"

_____

_____

_____

_____

_____

_____

_____

_____

_____

_____

TRANSFORMED: THE FRUIT OF THE SPIRIT

Now the Lord is the Spirit, and where the Spirit of the Lord is, there is freedom. And we all, with unveiled face, beholding the glory of the Lord, are being transformed into the same image from one degree of glory to another. For this comes from the Lord who is the Spirit.

2 Corinthians 3:17-18

DAY 15
SUNDAY
LIVING SACRIFICES
READ ROMANS 12:1-2

When you hear the word *sacrifice*, what comes to mind?

In our day and age, we may think of sacrifice as giving something up, such as when a father or mother sacrifices a lucrative career to spend more time with the family. The idea of sacrifice in the Bible does involve a measure of giving something up as an expression of love and devotion to God. That's a simple enough definition, yet it's inadequate.

In the Old Testament, animal sacrifice was a means of approaching the presence of God in worship. It was an expression of turning back to God after sin and rebellion. Other offerings in the Old Testament involved the sacrifice of crops and grains, or the gift of bread and wine representing a person's labor of love. These "thank offerings" were expressions of gratitude to the Lord in response to His blessing and abundant provision.

Sacrifices were necessary in the Old Testament because God's dwelling place was external to the people of God. His presence was manifested in the innermost chamber of the Old Temple, in the Holy of Holies. Because God is holy, sinful people could never get too close to His presence or they would be consumed. Barriers, walls, and curtains shielded God's presence to protect the people from the piercing light of his holiness and glory.

Offerings of slaughtered animals were made as a symbol of a sacrifice for sin. Yet these sacrifices gained the Jewish people only partial access to the presence of the Holy, Holy, Holy God—never full or complete access. And so, in a sense, the people were still hiding from God, just as Adam and Eve hid in the garden from the presence of God, ashamed of their sin.

The only person who ever entered into the Holy of Holies—where God's presence dwelled—was the high priest, and he only one time a year on the Day of Atonement. For the high priest to enter, an elaborate festival with multiple sacrifices had to take place and everything was done according to the letter of the law. The high priest even tied a rope around his leg in case, when he entered through the curtain into the Holy of Holies, he was deemed not worthy and consumed by God's glory. The rope ensured the people could pull him out without risking their own lives!

But everything changed with Jesus. His death on the Cross made final atonement for sin, once and for all. You will remember that on the day of the Crucifixion, at the moment Jesus breathed His last, the curtain of the temple was torn in two from top to bottom—the curtain that separated the people from the presence of God in the Holy of Holies. God Himself tore down the final barrier to His holy presence! The sacrifice of Jesus gave us full and complete access to the Father.

Before His death on the Cross, Jesus prophesied the destruction of the temple in Jerusalem and all its animal sacrifices. He declared that in three days, He would raise it again. The Gospel writer John adds a little note saying, *"The temple that he was talking about was his own body"* (John 2:21). The Scriptures declare that Jesus would build a New Temple with the living stones of His people whose lives are offered to Him as living sacrifices (1 Peter 2:5).

In the New Temple, bulls and goats are not offered. They are no longer necessary. Jesus has made a final atonement so that *"we may approach God's throne of grace with confidence"* (Hebrews 4:16, NIV) without fear, guilt, or shame. But in light of that final mercy and grace in the sacrifice of Jesus, there is still one sacrifice necessary—the living sacrifice of ourselves. Because of Jesus' sacrifice, we can boldly approach the throne of grace without fear, guilt, or shame and offer ourselves as living sacrifices.

The Apostle Paul talks about this idea of a living sacrifice:

I appeal to you therefore, brothers, by the mercies of God, to present your bodies as a living sacrifice, holy and acceptable to God, which is your spiritual worship. Do not be conformed to this world, but be transformed by the renewal of your mind, that by testing you may discern what is the will of God, what is good and acceptable and perfect.   **Romans 12:1-2**

If you read the Scriptures carefully, you will discover that the Lord never actually desired animal sacrifices in and of themselves: *"I do not delight in the blood of bulls, or of lambs, or of goats"* (Isaiah 1:11). But rather, it was always the living sacrifice He desired: *"The sacrifices of God are a broken spirit; a broken and contrite heart, O God, you will not despise"* (Psalm 51:17).

REFLECT:

Are you ready to offer yourself as a living sacrifice as part of the New Temple? Your transformation to a living sacrifice will encompass your entire being: the dedication of your body, the renewal of your mind, and the submission of your will to God. Through the Holy Spirit, you will be empowered to love God with all your heart, with all your mind, and with all your strength. Tell God now that you are ready to give yourself fully to Him as a living sacrifice.

_____

_____

_____

_____

_____

_____

_____

_____

_____

DAY 16
MONDAY
MAN: THE DWELLING PLACE OF GOD
READ EPHESIANS 2:18-22

Take a mirror outside on a bright day and aim it toward the sun. You will see brilliant reflected light. Turn it away from the sun's brightness, and the mirror darkens.

From the beginning, humanity was called to reflect—like a mirror—God's glory, displaying His attributes to the world. As such, we would bear His likeness on earth (Genesis 1:28). But with the fall of humanity, humanity turned away from the light of God, no longer reflecting His glory. The mirror at the heart of man was darkened.

Paul describes what happened:

For although they knew God, they did not honor him as God or give thanks to him, but they became futile in their thinking, and their foolish hearts were darkened. Claiming to be wise, they became fools, and exchanged the glory of the immortal God for images resembling mortal man and birds and animals and creeping things.
Romans 1:21-23

In the analogy of the mirror, the mirror must face the sun to reflect its light. For human beings, we must "face" God in worship to reflect His light. In fact, worshiping God is the primary activity human beings were created to do. But whether we are worshiping

God or not, we never stop worshiping. We may shift our gaze and exchange the worship of Almighty God for the worship of lesser objects. At those moments, we have *"exchanged the truth about God for a lie and worshiped and served the creature rather than the Creator"* (Romans 1:25).

The consequence of humanity's exchange in worship has been absolutely disastrous! When we shift our lives from loving God with our hearts, minds, and strength, every aspect of our beings is given over to corruption and evil.

Misaligned minds become debased. Our thinking becomes chaotic and futile, and the true meaning and purpose of all things is lost. Wisdom flies out the window as our choices become foolish, immature, and without understanding.

When our hearts are oriented away from God and His truth, our desires are no longer pure. A heart that does not desire God will desire the things of this world above all else. Lust, pride, and greed take over and drive our decisions. Passions of the flesh control how we use our bodies and pursue possessions—and how we see others' bodies and possessions.

The misaligned mind and disoriented heart give way to the debasing and degrading of the body (our strength) in immoral behavior. Bodies are used to express misaligned love and disordered passion in forms of sexual immorality and perversions. They may also be used as instruments of cruelty, abuse, and violence.

Apart from worship of the true God, all human integrity breaks down. Good becomes evil and evil becomes good, as the Apostle Paul warns:

They were filled with all manner of unrighteousness, evil, covetousness, malice. They are full of envy, murder, strife, deceit, maliciousness. They are gossips, slanderers, haters of God, insolent, haughty, boastful, inventors of evil, disobedient to parents, foolish, faithless, heartless, ruthless. Though they know God's righteous decree that those who practice such things deserve to die, they not only do them but give approval to those who practice them.   **Romans 1:29-32**

God would redeem and reverse all of the above!

Through the mercy of Jesus Christ, we are not only being reestablished as reflections of God's image and likeness, but He is literally putting His light and attributes inside us through the transforming power of the Holy Spirit. Before Jesus came, the best we could do was reflect God's light, and only then as shards of a cracked and splintered mirror. After our full transformation when Christ returns, we will radiate the glory of God like a city on a hill, a light that cannot be hidden!

Even now, worship in the New Temple of Christ's gathered people takes the form of transformed lives. And that transformation occurs because of the presence of God dwelling in the midst of us—in the renewed hearts of His people through the Holy Spirit. When the Old Temple served as the dwelling place of God on earth, the glory of God remained external to us. Now the dwelling place of God is in us! The people of God are the New Temple of God.

So then you are no longer strangers and aliens, but you are fellow citizens with the saints and members of the household of God, built on the foundation of the apostles and prophets, Christ Jesus himself being the cornerstone, in whom the whole structure, being joined together, grows into a holy temple in the Lord. In him you also are being built together into a dwelling place for God by the Spirit.
Ephesians 2:19-22

The promise of Jesus is that, in the heart of the New Temple, resides the Spirit of the living God. The Shekinah Glory of God would dwell in the people of God—not in a building made by hands, but in a living building, a living structure made of human beings. You and I display the light of God's glory as we align our hearts, minds, and souls in worship of Him and as His Spirit indwells us. As Jesus says to us, *"You are the light of the world"* (Matthew 5:14).

REFLECT:

Do you remember the words of the children's song, "This little light of mine, I'm gonna let it shine"? There is a powerful truth in that song. In and of ourselves, we do not have any light. But our light is actually the light of Jesus that we "let" shine through us. How? By allowing His Spirit to transform our minds, hearts, and strength to reflect His holy attributes. Ask the Lord Jesus Christ to make you a lantern today, shining His holy light in a dark world.

_____

_____

_____

_____

_____

_____

_____

_____

_____

DAY 17
TUESDAY
KILLING THE LIZARD
READ 2 CORINTHIANS 5:16-21

It may seem odd to have a discussion about the dedication of our physical bodies in a book about the Holy Spirit, in a chapter on inner transformation. However, the relationship between our bodies and the Spirit is critical.

One aim of spiritual transformation is a transfigured body. In our key verse of Romans 12:1, Paul's appeal is *"to present your bodies as a living sacrifice, holy and acceptable to God, which is your spiritual worship."* God made the human body to shine with the beauty of divine radiance as the temple of the living God.

There's a fascinating illustration in C.S. Lewis's book, *The Great Divorce.* Two types of beings are interacting: ghosts and angels. The ghosts are human beings who have died but are stuck in a place of indecision between heaven and hell. The angels are encouraging the ghosts to turn away from hell. To do this, they must confront the one thing that is preventing them from truly surrendering to Jesus and becoming the heavenly creatures they are meant to be.

One of the ghosts has a chatty, annoying lizard on his shoulder. In the allegory, the lizard represents this man's sexual lust, a sin that he secretly enjoys, yet at the same time is ashamed of.

The angel asks the ghost, regarding the lizard, "May I kill it?"

The ghost replies, "Well, there's time to discuss that later."

The angel says, "There is no time. May I kill it?"

As the angel approaches the ghost, the ghost begins to feel a sensation of burning: "Why, you're hurting me now."

The angel responds: "I never said it wouldn't hurt you. I said it wouldn't kill you."

Just as the ghost is about to let the angel kill the lizard, the lizard starts to go crazy and screeches to the man, "Be careful…He can do what he says. He can kill me. One fatal word from you and he will! Then you'll be without me for ever and ever. It's not natural. How could you live?"

As the angel continues to approach, the lizard becomes more and more agitated on the ghost's shoulder. Finally, in one decisive moment, the ghost surrenders to the angel. The angel grabs the lizard and twists it off the ghost's shoulder as the ghost screams, flinging the lizard to the ground.

 As soon as the lizard is gone, the ghost begins to transform into a solid being, stronger and more corporeal—a real man.

As the ghost transforms into the physical man he was intended to be, a fascinating change is happening to the lizard. It begins to transform too—into a mighty stallion upon which the man mounts and rides into heaven!

Powerful imagery—a wimpy, whispering (the lizard) tyrant becomes a powerful servant (a stallion) with the man's hard-wrought decision to surrender it to the Lord.

As Lewis writes:

> *"Nothing, not even the best and noblest, can go on as it now is. Nothing, not even what is lowest and most bestial, will not be raised again if it submits to death. It is sown a natural body, it is raised a spiritual body. Flesh and blood cannot come to the*

Mountains [heaven]. Not because they are too rank, but because they are too weak. What is a lizard compared with a stallion? Lust is a poor, weak, whimpering whispering thing compared with that richness and energy of desire which will arise when lust has been killed." [1]

In our contemporary culture, the lust that so insidiously reigns over us, feeding on the images displayed on our television, movie, and computer screens, constantly whispering into our lives, is making us into weak shadows of the true selves God made us to be. May we have eyes to see it for what it is and see what it is doing to us.

Because sin has been reigning in our lives by our own personal allowance or through the inheritance of a general corruption of human nature from the Fall, we have become shadows of who we are supposed to be in our physical beings. We are imprisoned in this ghostly state. What we desperately need is to have the sin nature killed in us so that we can be transformed into the beings we are called to be—more fully real.

The world wants to keep us the same, leaving our lizards intact (whatever they may be)—blessing them as if they were our true identity. The world would turn us into a shadow or vapor of our true selves.

But the Apostle Paul urges, *"Do not be conformed to the pattern of this world, but be transformed..."* (Romans 12:1).

Only God's Holy Spirit can destroy the sin that reigns over us and transform us into new creatures. If you allow it, the Holy Spirit will turn you into something more beautiful and more godly than who you are naturally. He will make you more fully human, more real.

REFLECT:

What is the "lizard" on your shoulder? Which activity, sin, or desire is keeping you from surrendering completely to Jesus? The Lord wants to transform you, as the angel did the ghost, into a more real creature, able to fulfill His purpose for your life. Don't listen to the lies of the lizard—you will not die without him! Ask God to kill the lizard and begin your stunning transformation into His strong and eternal creature.

_____

_____

_____

_____

_____

_____

_____

_____

_____

_____

DAY 18
WEDNESDAY
RENEWED MIND, REASONABLE WORSHIP
READ 1 CORINTHIANS 2:6-15

In our key passage, Romans 12:1-2, the Apostle Paul urges us to *"present your bodies as a living sacrifice, holy and acceptable to God, which is your spiritual worship."* What does Paul mean by spiritual worship?

In some English versions, the word "spiritual" is translated as "rational." The Greek word is **λογικός** (logikos) meaning "reasonable, rational." Of course, we get our word logical from this Greek word. But how does this idea connect with worship?

In the Great Commandment, we are called to love the Lord our God with all heart and with all our strength and with all our mind. That means our transformation will require a renewal of the mind as we learn God's wisdom. Through the years, one of the great tricks of Satan has been to deny the wisdom of God by substituting the cheap imitation of his own "logic."

"Did God actually say, 'You shall not eat of any tree in the garden'?" Satan asked Eve. And, *"For God knows that when you eat of it [the fruit of the tree of knowledge of good and evil]… you will be like God, knowing good and evil"* (Genesis 3:1,5). The devil's strategy has been to make fools of men and women by tricking us through lies and manipulation, doubt and temptation.

A.W. Tozer reflects on how the devil is actually Creation's greatest fool:

> *...for when he gambled on his ability to unseat the Almighty he was guilty of an act of judgment so bad as to be imbecilic. He is said to have had a great amount of wisdom, but his wisdom must have deserted him at the time of his first sin, for surely he greatly underestimated the power of God and as grossly overestimated his own. The devil is not now pictured in the Scriptures as wise, only as shrewd. We are warned not against his wisdom but against his wiles, something very different.* [2]

The Scriptures describe how we followed Satan's idiocy and our thinking became "futile" and our minds were "depraved" because we did not seek the knowledge of God. Like Satan, we claimed to be wise, but we became fools as we suppressed the plain truth about God and exchanged it for a lie (Romans 1:18-22).

In the world today, humanity is divided into two classes of people: the wise and the foolish. Those who claim to be wise in the world's ways consider the study of God to be the mental work of idiots and the simpleminded. *"The natural person does not accept the things of the Spirit of God, for they are folly to him, and he is not able to understand them because they are spiritually discerned"* (1 Corinthians 2:14).

According to the world's "wisdom," those who assert divine ethics, godly values, and moral truths are backwards, out of touch, or even prejudiced and evil. The higher you climb the ladder of "higher learning," the less you will study God. And if you are an academic in such a place, the more you will be ridiculed—even persecuted—if divine logic and Christ's authority are the central assumptions and starting points of your thought. Yet, in God's economy, it is the "simpleminded fools" the world derides who are truly wise.

The Scriptures ask:

Where is the one who is wise? Where is the scribe? Where is the debater of this age? Has not God made foolish the wisdom of the world? For since, in the wisdom of God, the world did not know God through wisdom, it pleased God through the folly of what we preach to save those who believe... For the foolishness of God is wiser than men, and the weakness of God is stronger than men.

1 Corinthians 1: 20-21, 25

And:

Do not conform to the pattern of this world, but be transformed by the renewing of your mind.   **Romans 12:2, NIV**

The redemption and renewal of the human mind is essential for our transformation into the likeness of Christ. That is how we gain true wisdom. But how are we to do this? By setting our minds on the things of God. As Paul writes: *"Set your minds on things that are above, not on things that are on earth"* (Colossians 3:2). Center your mind on Jesus Christ and Him crucified and raised as of first importance and the starting point for divine wisdom. Through the indwelling Holy Spirit, our thoughts must conform to the thoughts and mind of Christ.

For the Spirit searches everything, even the depths of God. For who knows a person's thoughts except the spirit of that person, which is in him? So also no one comprehends the thoughts of God except the Spirit of God. Now we have received not the spirit of the world, but the Spirit who is from God, that we might understand the things freely given us by God.   **1 Corinthians 2:11-12**

If we have the Spirit of God in us, which was also in Christ Jesus, we begin to discern step-by-step the mind of God. On the one hand, who could know the mind of God? Yet, Paul is arguing that, through the indwelling Spirit of God, our minds can be illuminated with His wisdom. *"For who has understood the mind of the Lord so as to instruct him? But we have the mind of Christ"* (1 Corinthians 2:16).

The first step to the renewal of our mind is to ask God for wisdom: *"If any of you lacks wisdom, let him ask God, who gives generously to all without reproach, and it will be given him"* (James 1:5).

We should ask God to illumine our minds and reveal His thoughts to us. This is something that we can do at any time and in any place. The Holy Spirit is ever present in the mind of the believer. We will know the wisdom of God when we see it—it bears the marks of divine attributes: *"But the wisdom from above is first pure, then peaceable, gentle, open to reason, full of mercy and good fruits, impartial and sincere"* (James 3:17-18).

Second, your mind must meditate day and night on the Word of God revealed in the Scriptures. The Scriptures themselves were not *"produced by the will of man, but men spoke from God as they were carried along by the Holy Spirit"* (2 Peter 1:21). We do well to devote serious attention to the Scriptures as to a *"light shining in a dark place until the day dawns and the morning star rises in your hearts"* (2 Peter 1:19).

For this reason, Paul instructs his young protégé, Timothy, that the Holy Scriptures are able to *"make you wise for salvation through faith in Christ Jesus"* (2 Timothy 3:15) because *"all Scripture is breathed out by God and profitable for teaching, for reproof, for correction, and for training in righteousness, that the man of God may be complete, equipped for every good work"* (2 Timothy 3:16).

In the offering of our minds to spiritual (reasonable) worship, we begin to understand the logic and wisdom of God for us and for this world. It's not a quick or simple thing. Such wisdom cannot be attained by one act or in an instant. It's a gradual step-by-step process of daily prayer, worship, reading, and studying that begins to familiarize us with the mind of Christ—a process that will continue through eternity. Through the twin spiritual practices of asking for wisdom and meditating on the wisdom of God revealed in the Holy Scriptures by His Spirit, our minds are renewed and our lives transformed.

REFLECT:

Whom do you consider truly wise in the ways of God? How does the world view this person? This week, make a practice of asking God for wisdom, beginning right now. Then, take time to meditate on the wisdom of God revealed in the Scriptures. Watch as your mind and your life are gradually transformed.

_____

_____

_____

_____

_____

_____

_____

_____

_____

_____

DAY 19
THURSDAY
RENEWED DESIRES

READ GALATIANS 5:16-26

I love my children, but I don't always enjoy having to make and enforce rules. Yet one of the goals of parenting is to help our children learn how to make wise choices and develop strong character. People do not come out of the womb fully formed. To help shape our children's character, we lay down rules:

Rule: You may use your electronic devices only an hour and thirty minutes a day.

Rule: You will take turns cleaning the dishes after dinner.

Rule: You must be ready to leave the house by 8:10 in the morning.

My oldest son is turning 16 this year and my wife found an 8-page contract of rules online to govern his driving habits!

Why do we govern children by rules and contracts? Because, in their immaturity, their wills are not strong enough to regulate their own behavior—or so we think. If there were not a rule against overindulgence in electronic devices, they would use them all day long, right?

But could we shepherd our children's hearts so that they would self-moderate? If there were not a rule about helping out in the kitchen, would they do so anyway if they had the right internal motivation to love their family and eschew self-centeredness?

Often teenagers who grow up in heavily-regulated homes go "wild" when they get to college, indulging their newfound freedom in the cornucopia of vices found on a college campus. But is it necessary that there be a rule for every good thing we would like to see in our lives or a law to eliminate every bad thing? The world's pattern is, at any given moment, to both create an excess of external laws to control every behavior deemed "unacceptable" while at the same time rebelling against every control of licentiousness and lawlessness.

We can create myriad laws and rules. We can fill up jails with individuals who take the works of the flesh to the extreme. But such rules and constraints have no power to actually transform the heart—they only regulate behaviors. Even for those who obey, the law may simply mask an unconverted heart. The deeper solution is transformation that comes only from freedom from the law joined with the transforming work of God's Holy Spirit.

Think about it: The fully transformed life would be a rule-free, law-free, sin-free life. Complete freedom, but without sin. How is this possible?

The prophets of the Old Testament looked forward to a day when the laws of God would be written on the human heart:

For this is the covenant that I will make with the house of Israel after those days, declares the Lord: I will put my law within them, and I will write it on their hearts. And I will be their God, and they shall be my people. And no longer shall each one teach his neighbor and each his brother, saying, 'Know the Lord,' for they shall all know me, from the least of them to the greatest, declares the Lord.

Jeremiah 31:33-34a

The Spirit-filled person needs no command or rule telling him the right way to go; his heart would internally govern him. The Lord's Spirit would instruct from within.

You see, the real test of whether the character of Christ is in us is not whether we follow the religious rules and laws well. The real test is, when the religious rules and laws are removed, do our hearts remain fixed on knowing and loving the Lord? The truth about a person's character is revealed not by what she does when she is compelled to do it, but by what she does when she is free to do whatever her heart desires. The heart is the key.

Ironically, even a life controlled by religious rules can mask an unredeemed, rebellious heart. This was Paul's concern for the Church in Galatia. Some were seeking to force the "legal badge" of the Jewish covenant onto Gentile converts. Circumcision was an external sign of being "set apart" from the world unto covenant with God. You can understand why there would be some hesitation on the part of an adult Gentile convert to undergo this ritual cutting!

Paul vigorously argues in his letter for the law-free life of Gospel freedom graciously given in Christ. He tells the Galatian Church that whether you follow the law and bear the mark of the badge or not, it doesn't affect your spiritual standing—the external, legalistic test of circumcision reveals nothing about the "internal badge" of a transformed heart! *"For in Christ Jesus neither circumcision nor uncircumcision counts for anything, but only faith working through love"* (Galatians 5:6).

Here is a place where those of us who follow sacramental practice and are liturgically-minded must be very thoughtful about our patterns of Christian formation. The outward signs of baptism, confirmation, communion, anointing, etc. are valuable to us as symbols and signs of spiritual renewal. They signify deep spiritual realities. But they can become mere rules and laws disconnected from God's grace and internal spiritual change.

Christian formation is not about making sure we check off all the religious boxes on our heavenly entrance form. It is about making sure our hearts are aligned with the heart of God, revealed in Jesus Christ.

For the desires of the flesh are against the Spirit, and the desires of the Spirit are against the flesh, for these are opposed to each other, to keep you from doing the things you want to do. But if you are led by the Spirit, you are not under the law. **Galatians 5:17-18**

The Holy Spirit convicts the hearts of believers so that they know when they are not walking in the Spirit, for the works of the flesh are obvious: *"sexual immorality, impurity, sensuality, idolatry, sorcery, enmity, strife, jealousy, fits of anger, rivalries, dissensions, divisions, envy, drunkenness, orgies, and things like these"* (Galatians 5:19-21). There is always the danger that the free person may imperil his freedom by small choices to gratify the passions of the flesh that are destructive of that freedom.

The key to ultimate change is the conversion of the heart. Your call is to put to death the desires that lead to such works through keeping in step with the Spirit. *"Those who belong to Christ Jesus have crucified the flesh with its passions and desires"* (Galatians 5:24).

"But the fruit of the Spirit is love, joy, peace, patience, kindness, goodness, faithfulness, gentleness, self-control; against such things there is no law" (Galatians 5:22-23). You never have to put a hedge around having too much love. Joy and peace need no regulation to keep them in check in your life. Nor is the fruit of the Spirit accomplished in your life by external mandate. The Spirit governs by the internal constraint of love.

Our challenge in our maturity, then, is to learn how to walk by the Spirit and not simply be compelled by laws. Laws and rules are helpful to prescribe a general pattern of behavior—like a schoolteacher educating children. But the mature believer will live for

God with no need for a legalistic guide. A child is taught to paint by numbers and color inside the lines. But an adult artist knows internally the rules of color, depth, and perspective, can create from the minimal constraints of a blank canvas, and paints a magnificent work of art, beautiful in form and splendid in design.

REFLECT:

Freedom does not mean that we gratify the desires of the sin nature, like law-bound children released to college hedonism. Rather, real freedom means that the Spirit of God takes over the job of self-regulation and we walk in the desires of the Spirit. Do you have that kind of freedom in your life? Ask the Lord to enable you to walk by His Spirit and you will not seek to satisfy the desires of the flesh. You will be truly free!

DAY 20
FRIDAY
TRANSFIGURED

READ 2 CORINTHIANS 3:12-18

One of the more important, yet mysterious, events that happened in the life of Jesus was the journey He took with three of His closest disciples up onto a "high mountain" where His appearance was completely changed before their eyes:

And after six days Jesus took with him Peter and James and John, and led them up a high mountain by themselves. And he was trans-figured before them, and his clothes became radiant, intensely white, as no one on earth could bleach them.　　**Mark 9:2-4**

Jesus went through a complete metamorphosis before Peter, James, and John, becoming radiant as the sun, His clothes turning bright-er than any imaginable white. For a brief moment, Jesus pulled back the veil and revealed His true character and divine nature as the Son of God. These three disciples were given a temporary glimpse of the greater light of His glory, and it was magnificent! Peter wanted to build tents and remain on the mountain.

The Greek word used to describe what happened to Jesus is translat-ed "transfigured." And so we commonly refer to Jesus' transfigura-tion. But the word is used four times in the New Testament—twice in reference to Jesus' transfiguration (Matthew 17:2 and Mark 9:2) and twice in reference to something that happens to us (Romans 12:2 and 2 Corinthians 3:18). Why have you not heard about *your* transfiguration before now? Because, in those latter two instances, the English translators have chosen the word "transformed" instead of "transfigured"—but it is the same word. Whether we say transfigured or transformed, it is the same word in the original Greek text: μεταμορφόω, *metamorphoó.* We get our word "metamorphosis" from it.

The two verses in Scripture that describe our transfiguration are:

Do not be conformed to this world, but be transformed (metamorphosized, transfigured) *by the renewal of your mind.*
Romans 12:2

And,

And we all, with unveiled face, beholding the glory of the Lord, are being transformed (metamorphosized, transfigured) into the same image from one degree of glory to another. For this comes from the Lord who is the Spirit. **2 Corinthians 3:18**

So the transformation that is taking place in us is that we are being transfigured into the image of God and into the character of Jesus Christ.

This transformation begins with the consecration of our bodies to be the dwelling place of God's Spirit. It is followed by the renewing of our minds and the realignment of our hearts' desires, resulting in the manifestation of His glory in us: transfiguration!

CONSECRATED BODY → RENEWED MIND → REALIGNED HEART → TRANSFIGURATION

We know that we are being transfigured when we begin to see the fruit of the Spirit in our lives: love, joy, peace, patience, kindness, goodness, faithfulness, gentleness, and self-control. They work their way out from the Spirit dwelling in our heart. They begin to become character traits in us so that our actions are no longer determined by what's happening in the world. We have love even when our enemies don't love us and are persecuting us. We have peace when we're being threatened. We have joy in the midst of difficult circumstances.

You know, Paul is in prison when he writes, *"Rejoice in the Lord always; again I will say, rejoice"* (Philippians 4:4). He's contemplating his own death and yet he is calling upon the Church to be filled with joy. The way Paul looks at it, because of his chains, the whole Roman prison guard is coming to know Jesus. Isn't that wonderful?

His joy is not stolen by circumstances. Why? Because he isn't a chameleon. But Paul's reactions are not "colored" by his circumstances. He doesn't change with the company he's hanging around. Chameleons, they switch; they're conformed to whatever group or "color" they're around. His life is governed by the Spirit of God and his character has been transformed by the living God. So no matter where he is in the world, no matter what's happening to him, he will be of the same character.

Some people stay away from church because they've seen hypocrites—people who are nice and loving at church, but go home to their families or workplaces, and are abusive, mean, dishonest, or immoral. That's not a person who has been transformed. That's a lizard, a chameleon, who is merely conforming to the Church environment as a temporary "color change."

But for people who are truly transformed, it doesn't matter which group of people they're with or what circumstances they're in. They will manifest the character of God in and out of season, with this group or that group, with Christians or pagans—anybody. They are the same at home as in public. Their character remains steady.

The pressure is upon you daily to be a chameleon. Resist it and draw near to the Lord! For there is a greater transformational power at work within you, shaping and forming you to bear the image of God to the world. God would see His character displayed in you. The Holy Spirit is transfiguring you to shine with the light of His glory in a dark world.

REFLECT:

We often associate "peer pressure" with teenagers, but it is a challenge for all of us. When have you found yourself conforming to a group of people or situation rather than being transformed into the image of Christ? How did it make you feel? In what ways do you see yourself becoming transfigured by the Spirit daily? What specific fruit of the Spirit would you like God to manifest in your life this week? Ask Him now.

_____

_____

_____

_____

_____

_____

_____

_____

_____

_____

DAY 21
SATURDAY
THE WAY OF LOVE IS PRIMARY
READ 1 CORINTHIANS 13:1-13

One of the most popular Scripture passages for weddings is 1 Corinthians 13, often called the Love Chapter. But in the context of the letter to the Corinthian Church, this passage has a point not often considered.

The book of 1 Corinthians was written to a group of Christians who saw themselves as "spiritual" and gifted. But in actual practice, they were quite worldly, especially in the way they were acting toward one another. Their fellowship was riddled with self-centered divisions and arrogance. They lacked the most important quality: love.

There is a great little book called *The Greatest Thing in the World*, written by Henry Drummond. In it, the author identifies two classes of sins that plague the human race: sins of the body and sins of the disposition.

Take the story of the prodigal son. The younger brother—the prodigal—certainly manifested the sins of the body. But of equal concern in the story are the sins of the disposition exhibited by the elder brother. Drummond writes:

> *The peculiarity of ill temper is that it is the vice of the virtuous. It is often the one blot on an otherwise noble character. You know men who are all but perfect, and women who would be entirely perfect,*

but for an easily ruffled, quick-tempered, or "touchy" disposition.... No form of vice, not worldliness, not greed of gold, not drunkenness itself, does more to un-Christianize society than evil temper. For embittering life, for breaking up communities, for destroying the most sacred relationships, for devastating homes, for withering up men and women, for taking the bloom of childhood, in short, FOR SHEER GRATUITOUS MISERY-PRODUCING POWER, this influence stands alone. [3]

Love is the operative word of the great commandment: *"'Love the Lord your God with all your heart and with all your soul and with all your strength and with all your mind;' and, 'Love your neighbor as yourself'"* (Matthew 22:37-38). Love is also first on the list of the fruit of the Spirit. And the Apostle Peter wrote, *"above all things have fervent love for one another"* (1 Peter 4:8, NKJV). Above all things! Love is the most important attribute for your life—it is the secret key to the Christian life. Yet, among the religious, the virtuous, the holy, the righteous ones, those who claim the name of Christ, it is often the one thing sorely lacking!

Jesus manifested love perfectly. Every place you find the word "love" in 1 Corinthians 13, you could substitute the name of Jesus. "Jesus is patient, Jesus is kind, Jesus does not envy, Jesus does not boast..." Out of all the people who ever lived, He manifested love in His life perfectly through the multitude of small acts and gestures He engaged in. Indeed this is how character is lived out—in small virtuous acts, consistently done.

Take one of the traits of love described in 1 Corinthians 13: patience. Jesus is patient. Over and over again, when His disciples failed or even betrayed Him, He restored them. Peter's denials and restoration comes to mind. Or take the trait of kindness. Jesus is kind. Do you remember how he healed the sick, touched the untouchable, restored the fallen and broken? He showed kindness to the woman at the well in Samaria and the blind beggar on the road to Jericho. Everywhere Jesus went, He displayed kindness and generosity.

Jesus does not envy. Jesus does not boast. He was offered all of the kingdoms of the world by Satan and yet would not claim the right to rule the world Satan's way. His only boast was in the Cross. Jesus is not arrogant or rude. He does not insist on His own way. He encouraged His disciples not to "lord it over" as the Gentile rulers do, but to emulate Him, *"for the Son of Man came not to be served but to serve, and to give his life as a ransom for many"* (Matthew 20:25-28).

Henry Drummond describes what he calls "The Spectrum of Love" as having nine ingredients:

Patience
  "Love suffereth long."

Kindness
  "And is kind."

Generosity
  "Love envieth not."

Humility
  "Love vaunteth not itself, is not puffed up."

Courtesy
  "Doth not behave itself unseemly."

Unselfishness
  "Seeketh not its own."

Good temper
  "Is not provoked."

Guilelessness
  "Taketh not account of evil."

Sincerity
  "Rejoiceth not in unrighteousness, but rejoiceth with the truth." [4]

"Patience; kindness; generosity; humility; courtesy; unselfishness; good temper; guilelessness; sincerity—these make up the supreme gift, the stature of the perfect man [or woman]." These are the ingredients of love. [5]

Every single phrase in this wonderful definition of love applies perfectly to Jesus. We can think of example after example in His life where He showed these attributes for us and to us. Jesus is the supreme example of the most excellent way of love.

Here is the turn: that we would be like Him in every way. His character becomes our character. His love is to manifest inside of us!

A real test of our growth and maturity in the transformation process is to put your name in place of the word love. Fill in every blank with your first name and say each phrase out loud. See whether it rings true or… is it laughable?

_____ is patient;

_____ is kind;

_____ does not envy;

_____ does not boast;

_____ is not arrogant;

_____ is not rude;

_____ does not insist on his/her own way;

_____ is not irritable;

_____ is not resentful;

_____ does not rejoice at wrongdoing,

but _____ rejoices with the truth.

_____ bears all things,

_____ believes all things,

_____ hopes all things,

_____ endures all things.

This is an exercise that can help us honestly evaluate our own maturity. When we are children, we act like children, we think like children. But as adults, we have to put childish ways behind us (1 Corinthians 13:11). Being an adult means manifesting love. When you wrote your name in the list above, was there any place where it didn't seem to fit? Was there a phrase that you read with an uncomfortable chuckle? Did you have a hard time reading your name on any line at all?

It is okay to be honest in this moment between you and the Lord. This is the place and time to do it. We all fall short and have growing up yet to do. And God knows it. He will help you grow in love as you acknowledge the areas where you need His help.

Your life is to be characterized by love, so that when others think of your name, the first word that comes to mind is love. Thinking back to the Church at Corinth, the deeper teaching of 1 Corinthians 13, the Love Chapter, is that this quality—love—is more important than any other gift you possess! It matters more than any other character trait you have, no matter how wonderful. If this one divine attribute is lacking in your life—if love is missing—then all else is for nothing, means nothing, and indeed gains nothing.

REFLECT:

Other than Jesus, whose name comes to mind when you think of the word "love" or "loving"? How does this individual show love to those around them? What qualities of love described in 1 Corinthians 13 do you already possess? Which ones do you need to grow in? Ask Jesus—the source and definition of LOVE—to help you today. You can become more loving! In fact, as Jesus transforms you, you will. But you must be willing.

_____

_____

_____

_____

_____

_____

_____

_____

_____

EQUIPPED: THE GIFTS OF THE SPIRIT

AND HE GAVE THE APOSTLES, THE PROPHETS, THE EVANGELISTS, THE SHEPHERDS AND TEACHERS, TO EQUIP THE SAINTS FOR THE WORK OF MINISTRY, FOR BUILDING UP THE BODY OF CHRIST, UNTIL WE ALL ATTAIN TO THE UNITY OF THE FAITH AND OF THE KNOWLEDGE OF THE SON OF GOD, TO MATURE MANHOOD, TO THE MEASURE OF THE STATURE OF THE FULLNESS OF CHRIST…
EPHESIANS 4:11-13

DAY 22
SUNDAY
THE GIFTS OF JESUS

READ ROMANS 12:4-8

Who doesn't like to receive a gift?

Jesus compared God to human fathers who love to give "good gifts" to their children when asked. He tells us that God the Father will graciously give the Holy Spirit as a good gift to those who seek and ask for it (Luke 11:13). While we can talk about the Holy Spirit as the big gift given to all Christians, the New Testament also talks about unique and individual endowments—gifts—given specifically and diversely to individual Christians.

This week, we are going to look at what it means to be equipped with the gifts of the Holy Spirit. In the New Testament, there are actually two Greek words translated as the English word "gift"— the words *charisma* and *dórea*. These two words are used interchangeably and almost synonymously in the Greek text of the Scriptures. In English, we use the one word, "gift."

Just as physical gifts can be neglected, squandered, misused, and abused, so too can spiritual gifts be poorly stewarded and even used for evil or selfish purposes. God gives us gifts that they may be used for His glory and purposes, in the service of His people. So here we come to a good definition of a spiritual gift: a spiritual gift is a unique and special endowment that is freely given to an individual believer by the Holy Spirit under the Lordship of Jesus Christ for the purpose of the growth, maturity, and vitality of the body of Christ, the Church. In other words, spiritual gifts are for serving.

In the letters of the Apostle Paul, we find three places where spiritual gifts are listed and discussed: Romans 12, 1 Corinthians 12-14, and Ephesians 4. Depending on how you organize them, the gifts are:

Romans 12
Exhortation • Giving • Leadership • Mercy • Prophecy • Service • Teaching

1 Corinthians 12-14
Administration • Discernment • Faith • Healing • Helps • Knowledge • Miracles • Tongues • Interpretation • Wisdom • Hospitality • Martyrdom • Missionary • Celibacy • Marriage

Ephesians 4
Apostle • Evangelist • Pastor • Prophet • Teacher

However, Paul's letters are not the only place where we read about the gifts of the Holy Spirit.

If you really want to understand and see the gifts of the Spirit in action, read the Gospels' stories about Jesus, the Anointed One. Filled with the Holy Spirit, Jesus exercised and manifested all the gifts of the Spirit. In fact, you can find examples in the Gospels of Jesus exercising each and every one of the gifts listed above. For example, Jesus administered a mighty movement; He healed and performed miracles; He spoke words of knowledge, wisdom, and exhortation; He was a prophet mighty in word and deed; He showed mercy and served others; He lived celibately. Jesus was the consummate host, showing hospitality by turning water into wine, feeding five thousand, and finally offering the bread and wine of His own body and blood. He had every gift; they are all Jesus' gifts.

Last week we looked at how we as individual Christians are all called to manifest *all* of the fruit of the Holy Spirit. The fruit of the Holy Spirit is actually the character of Jesus Christ—love, joy, peace, patience, kindness, goodness, faithfulness, gentleness, and self-control. Every follower of Jesus is called to display all the fruit of the Holy Spirit. It's not okay for a Christian to say, "I don't need the fruit of love." Or, "I don't seem to have the fruit of patience," or "Self-control is optional." Every Christian is called to manifest *every* fruit of the character of Christ.

But when it comes to the gifts of the Holy Spirit, they are uniquely given to individual Christians. No one Christian has all the gifts of the Spirit, as Jesus did. The gifts of the Holy Spirit are actually the gifts of Jesus given to us, distributed to each Christian individually.

So, what is the reason for the division of these various gifts among the members of the Church? In Ephesians 4:12-16, where Paul gives the reason for the gifts, he writes:

But each of us was given grace according to the measure of Christ's gift. Therefore it is said, "When he ascended on high he made captivity itself a captive; he gave gifts to his people." …The gifts he gave were that some would be apostles, some prophets, some evangelists, some pastors and teachers, to equip the saints for the work of ministry, for building up the body of Christ, until all of us come to the unity of the faith and of the knowledge of the Son of God, to maturity, to the measure of the full stature of Christ.   **Ephesians 4:7-8, 11-14 (NRSV)**

So the idea is that the Lord Jesus has given His gifts to believers, but has distributed them individually. This diversity of gifts given to His people requires us to work together in concert like a symphony made up of a variety of musical instruments creating a masterpiece together.

When Jesus ascended on high, He continued to administer the ministry He personally began in Galilee, but now on a wider scale. The gifts given to us are an extension of His ministry on earth. This is so critical to understand that it bears repeating: *the gifts we have been given are an extension of what Jesus was doing and is continuing to do on earth.* We are the instruments of that ministry and service. What a holy privilege and blessing to be given good gifts to be used in the service of God's people, for His glory!

GOD GIVES US GIFTS THAT THEY
MAY BE USED FOR HIS GLORY
AND PURPOSES, IN THE SERVICE
OF HIS PEOPLE.

REFLECT:

Reread the above lists of the Holy Spirit's gifts. Think about how Jesus used these gifts in His earthly ministry, such as healing, mercy, wisdom, service, and knowledge. How have these gifts of God been used to minister to you? Which gifts has God given you? How are you using these gifts to serve God's people?

_____

_____

_____

_____

_____

_____

_____

_____

_____

_____

DAY 23
MONDAY
SPIRITUAL GIFTS VS. SPIRITUAL MATURITY
READ 1 CORINTHIANS 12:27-13:3

Yesterday we learned that there are two Greek words in the New Testament that are translated as the English word, "gift"—*dórea* and *charisma*.

While believers often use the word *gift* to speak of the Holy Spirit's endowments, we may use the word *charisma* to talk about a special gifting of the Holy Spirit. Even in our non-religious vocabulary, we may say that a person has a charismatic personality or a particular charisma. What we are saying is that an individual has a certain "giftedness" that is special and unique.

For example, by "charismatic leader," we mean someone who has qualities that compel others to follow because of their natural giftings and talents. A charismatic leader may be an individual who is a great public speaker or has an attractive appearance or mannerism. He or she may be smart, humorous, or a gifted storyteller. In other words, a charismatic leader has some gift or endowment that stands out as exceptional. But such giftedness does not necessarily translate into strong leadership qualities.

Way too often we hear about pastors who reached "rock star status" because of a giftedness in preaching only to fall from grace due to some moral failure, often adultery. Experience and wisdom teach us that charismatic personalities are very gifted people, but they are not necessarily mature or equipped to serve as spiritual leaders. Charisma joined with immature or corrupt character is a dangerous combination.

The people in Corinth were very interested in spiritual gifts. They asked the Apostle Paul several questions about gifts and their importance. But Paul used the occasion of their questions to speak instead about their common life as a community. One of the main lessons Paul drove home to the Corinthian believers was that being spiritually gifted doesn't mean you're spiritually mature. And so, while 1 Corinthians chapters 12 and 14 are about spiritual gifts, chapter 13 is about spiritual maturity.

"But wait," you say. "Isn't 1 Corinthians 13 about love?"

Well, yes. First Corinthians 13 is a famous passage that talks about love and is often read at weddings. But it was written in the context of a discussion about spiritual gifts. Many of the problems the Corinthians were experiencing came from using their spiritual gifts *without* love! Paul challenges them to exercise their gifts with and through love—what he calls a *"more excellent way"* (1 Corinthians 12:31).

Let's break this down a bit. Paul begins, *"If I speak in the tongues of men and angels..."* because the Corinthian believers were very interested in the spiritual gift of speaking in tongues. Paul points out that, if you have the gift of speaking in tongues but you don't have love surrounding it, that gift is just a noisy gong or a clanging symbol—it's loud, irritating, and doesn't bless anyone! A verse later, Paul continues, *"And if I have a faith that can move mountains,"* which is a spiritual gift, *"but do not have love, I am nothing."* Faith that is powerful, yet without love, doesn't actually accomplish anything for the Church.

So the main point is, being spiritually gifted is not the same thing as being spiritually mature. Serving others through love is the whole point of the gifts—not showing off the gifts for one's own glory.

One of the big issues the Corinthian Church was facing—and this was caused by their lack of spiritual maturity—was divisions among them due to how they valued spiritual gifts. Not all Christians have the same gifts. The believers in Corinth were prizing some gifts above others, the more "glitzy gifts," like speaking in tongues (which can come across as ecstatic utterances) were believed to be more spiritual. Paul is saying that, just because you don't speak in tongues, that doesn't mean you are in any way less spiritual than a person who does. In fact, speaking in tongues is one of the lesser gifts; it doesn't really do a whole lot for the body of Christ without the interpretation of tongues to go along with it.

So then, a spiritual gift is not an end unto itself. It is not given to make you "lord" over other people—and I've seen this happen when someone has the gift of prophecy or of healing. Because some gifts are considered more "important" or "powerful" than other gifts, people with such gifts are in danger of becoming an island unto themselves, lacking the checks and balances that God has given to the body of Christ to keep gifts like prophecy and healing in check. These individuals may begin to go off and do their own thing, which can quickly get out of order and become hurtful because it's not brought under the submission of the body of Christ.

I was at a healing conference with Judith McNutt at the Christian Healing Ministry in Jacksonville, Florida, and Judith said a very interesting thing. She said, "I get asked all the time by people, 'Would you please pray that I would get the gift of speaking in tongues' or the gift of healing or prophecy?" Then she went on, "Nobody ever asks me for the fruit of the Holy Spirit." That's interesting, isn't it?

What Paul is saying is that it's good to eagerly strive for the gifts—we should ask for the gifts and seek them for the body. But, he says,

"I will show you a more excellent way" (1 Corinthians 12:31). That more excellent way is: pursue love, then strive for the gifts. Love is always first. And if you're not exercising the gifts in the context of love, then what you're doing is not of God.

While spiritual gifts are very important for the body of Christ, the way of love is the context in which the spiritual gifts are to be exercised. If we don't put the fruit of the Spirit, especially love, over the gifts of the Spirit, we have things out of order. When we put love first, all the gifts thrive among God's people.

AND IF I HAVE A FAITH THAT CAN
MOVE MOUNTAINS, BUT DO NOT HAVE
LOVE, I AM NOTHING.

1 CORINTHIANS 13:2

REFLECT:

When have you witnessed a gift of the Holy Spirit being exercised without love? What was the result? Ask the Lord today to first give you love for others and then to help you exercise your spiritual gift in that powerful context.

_____

_____

_____

_____

_____

_____

_____

_____

_____

_____

DAY 24
TUESDAY
CONFLICT OVER GIFTS
READ 1 CORINTHIANS 12:1-13

Jesus has ascended on high and has given gifts to men for the administration of His body on earth. That means that all spiritual gifts are to be under the Lordship of Jesus Christ. It's His Spirit that is being poured out and all gifts come from Him.

The Apostle Paul writes in 1 Corinthians, chapter 12:

Now concerning spiritual gifts, brothers and sisters, I do not want you to be uninformed. You know that when you were pagans, you were enticed and led astray to idols that could not speak. Therefore I want you to understand that no one speaking by the Spirit of God ever says, "Let Jesus be cursed!" and no one can say, "Jesus is Lord" except by the Holy Spirit. **1 Corinthians 12:1-3 (NRSV)**

Right out of the gate, Paul wants to make sure we understand that just because something is spiritual doesn't mean it's truly of the Holy Spirit. One of the primary tests of whether something is really of the Holy Spirit is its submission to the Lordship of Christ. This is critically important to understand! If a gift or a spiritual experience does not point to Jesus Christ as Lord, it is not of His Spirit.

We have people in our day and age—Oprah is a great example—who love all things spiritual. If it's spiritual, Oprah's going to have it on her show and encourage people to try it. But if the spirit that is being invited to speak into your life doesn't submit to the Lordship of Jesus Christ, it's not the Holy Spirit! Paul gives the example of the pagan background of the Corinthians. He says, *"You were enticed and led astray to idols that could not speak"* (1 Corinthians 12:2, NRSV). There are false gods and spiritual powers at work in this world. We need to stay aware of this reality. Just because it's spiritual doesn't mean it's "Holy Spirited." The Holy Spirit doesn't deny or ignore Jesus; He always exalts Jesus Christ as Lord.

Spiritual gifts not only must be tested to determine if they are truly of the Holy Spirit, but they also need to be practiced humbly and under the administration of the Church. Conflict over spiritual gifts often comes when someone with a particular gift asserts its dominance to the exclusion or minimization of others, or practices the gift as a "solo" player outside the oversight of God's people.

I saw this happen with a minister who had the gift of healing. This pastor was definitely gifted and God had healed many people through his ministry. But there was an occasion when he came to my congregation in a spirit of arrogance and attempted to exercise his gift without seeking my permission as the pastor or working in concert with the gifts of the other members of our local body. In a sense, he behaved as if his gift was superior to the gifts of others, such as discernment. So without discerning the context of one family's struggle, he spoke words to them regarding healing with no knowledge or pastoral understanding as if they were directly from the Lord. Rather than build this family up, the man caused tremendous damage.

The same thing was happening in Corinth. Certain members were exalting some gifts as super-spiritual, such as a speaking in tongues (even though that gift was one of the least important for the building up of the body of Christ, which is the ultimate purpose of the gifts). Paul uses the occasion to remind the believers at Corinth that not everybody has the same spiritual gift, and we need to be careful in our exercise and evaluation of spiritual gifts. We need to know their purpose, recognize that there's a diversity of them, and understand the reason for that diversity.

What is that reason? Well, the diverse distribution of gifts forces the members of the Church to work together. The Church needs all the gifts to function robustly in its mission and ministry. Paul uses the imagery of the human body with its various interdependent parts. All the parts of the body are necessary for the whole body's healthy functioning, and all parts require the others to work effectively. The gifts of the Spirit are like parts of the body—they are mutually interdependent, needing each other and working together to keep the body healthy.

This was the problem in the example I gave above. The gift of healing is a blessing to the Church and needed by the body; however, it needs to be exercised in concert with the pastoral gifts, as well as the gifts of discernment of spirits and prophecy. The man with the gift of healing was acting in isolation from the other gifts and, therefore, his work was not only ineffective, it was damaging.

There's a unity within the diversity of gifts that results from the Lordship of Jesus Christ over the gifts and the Holy Spirit as the giver of all gifts. So divisions over spiritual gifts don't make sense. Even though the believers at Corinth thought of themselves as very spiritual because of their charisma (giftedness), they weren't being very spiritual in the way they were exercising those gifts. This is Paul's point:

There are diversities of gifts, but the same Spirit... But the manifestation of the Spirit is given to each one for the profit of all: for to one is given the word of wisdom through the Spirit, to another the word of knowledge through the same Spirit, to another faith by the same Spirit, to another gifts of healings by the same Spirit, to another the working of miracles, to another prophecy, to another discerning of spirits, to another different kinds of tongues, to another the

*interpretation of tongues. But one
and the same Spirit works all these
things, distributing to each one individually as He wills.*

   1 Corinthians 12: 1-11 (NKJV)

We can create a long list of gifts
from this passage. But Paul reminds us that all of these gifts are
from the same source—the Holy
Spirit—and that the Spirit gives
different gifts to different people.
Not everyone gets the same gift.
Whose prerogative is it to give the
gifts? The Spirit's! It's not something you can decide for yourself. The Holy Spirit gives gifts as
He wills. That's one reason they
are called "gifts," because they are
freely given by the Spirit.

Another reason they are called
"gifts" is because they are not
something we can buy or earn.
In the book of Acts, there was a
man named Simon who tried to
buy the gift of bestowing the Holy
Spirit from the apostles:

*Now when Simon saw that the
Spirit was given through the lay-
ing on of the apostles' hands,
he offered them money, saying, "Give me this power also,
so that anyone on whom I lay
my hands may receive the Holy*

**THE CHURCH
NEEDS ALL
THE GIFTS
TO FUNCTION
ROBUSTLY IN ITS
MISSION AND
MINISTRY.**

Spirit.” But Peter said to him, “May your silver perish with you, because you thought you could obtain the gift of God with money!” **Acts 8:18-20**

No, the Holy Spirit is not something we can buy or control. It is freely given. The same is true of the Spirit's gifts, whether healing, prophecy, hospitality, faith, discernment of spirits, teaching, and so on. They are all gifts. So let's be thankful for the gifts we have and use them to encourage the body of Christ.

REFLECT:

When have you come across an experience or practice that was "spiritual" but not of the Holy Spirit? How could you tell? Have you ever desired a gift of the Holy Spirit that you don't have? It's okay to ask God for that gift, but remember that the Spirit ultimately gives us the needed gifts to best serve the believers around us.

_____

_____

_____

_____

_____

_____

_____

_____

_____

_____

DAY 25
WEDNESDAY
GIFTS AND THE BODY
READ 1 CORINTHIANS 12:14-31

Now you are the body of Christ and individually members of it. And God has appointed in the Church first apostles, second prophets, third teachers, then miracles, then gifts of healing, helping, administrating, and various kinds of tongues. Are all apostles? Are all prophets? Are all teachers? Do all work miracles? Do all possess gifts of healing? Do all speak with tongues? Do all interpret? But earnestly desire the higher gifts. And I will show you a still more excellent way.   **1 Corinthians 12:27-31**

Paul connects the gifts of the Holy Spirit to the resurrected body of Christ. He uses this metaphor "the body of Christ"—and I think it's more than a metaphor; we truly are the resurrected body of Christ on earth—because there's a diversity of gifts, and bodies, too, have a diversity of parts that enable them to function in life and stay healthy.

Do you hear what Paul is saying about the different parts of the body in verses 14-20 of today's reading? They have various functions. And the functions of those parts, from the more visible parts such as hands and eyes to the invisible parts such as brains, hearts, and livers, all serve to help the body live, mature, and grow. So it is with the Church. Different members of the body all have special roles to play. They are different roles, yet they're all necessary in order for the body to be healthy, growing, and maturing under the head, which is Jesus Christ. Every member is critical!

When I was attending the University of Florida, I had a roommate named Dan who was studying to be a doctor. I learned more from Dan about the human body than I really wanted to know! On one occasion he began to list all the parts of the body that a person can live without. You could probably come up with some of them. Your spleen, appendix, tonsils—those are the easy ones. But Dan listed other things. For example, you don't really need your hands or your eyes. There are people who exist without their tongues. You don't really need your ears. (In fact, if you're married, your spouse probably wonders at times if you still have them!) If you think about it, we can eliminate quite a few parts of our bodies and still live.

But what ends up happening if you don't have these parts? Such a body may be able to exist, but it lacks something. It cannot live as fully as it was designed to live. Many brave individuals are living very full lives with arms or legs missing, or eyes or ears that don't function. But they would be the first to say that their body is missing something. It is impaired. As such, it is unable to do some of the things bodies were designed to do.

The Church is designed like a body with myriad members and parts, each with a unique function and role to play for the building up of the larger whole. When every member does its part and works in harmony and concert with the other members, the body flourishes and thrives with abundant life. The Lord delights to see his Church functioning in a healthy and mature way with each member playing his or her role.

But just as you can survive and function without legs or eyes, the Church can continue without key spiritual gifts being exercised too. However, when a member's gift is not being exercised, the

Church body is diminished and impaired in significant ways. The Apostle Paul writes:

If the foot should say, "Because I am not a hand, I do not belong to the body," that would not make it any less a part of the body. And if the ear should say, "Because I am not an eye, I do not belong to the body," that would not make it any less a part of the body. If the whole body were an eye, where would be the sense of hearing? If the whole body were an ear, where would be the sense of smell? But as it is, God arranged the members in the body, each one of them, as he chose.   **1 Corinthians 12:15-18**

Paul is addressing what you might call insecurity on the part of some members because they're not the glitzier body parts. *"On the contrary,"* Paul writes, *"the members of the body that seem to be weaker are indispensable"* (1 Corinthians 12:22). Spleens are good. Paul's also addressing arrogance on the part of others who think of themselves more highly than they ought.

As a teacher, my spiritual gift is pretty visible. The temptation might be for a layperson to think, "Because I am not up front teaching and preaching like the pastor, I am not very important." Conversely, I could think with pride, "Well, you know, I'm the teacher, so I'm the most important." Paul says both estimations are wrong. We are not to think of ourselves as second-class or sub-spiritual because we don't have the same spiritual gift as another person, nor are we to puff ourselves up because of our gift.

One weekend, we had a special visit from our bishop. It was amazing to see so many of our members using their gifts. One member, Evelisse, exercised her gift of hospitality by serving as the reception hostess. Another, Nancy, made beautiful floral decorations, with Norma's help. Rick washed dishes. Ross, our bookkeeper, made sure the bills were paid, and Susie administered the entire affair. If everyone had worked on the floral arrangements, we wouldn't have had any food. If Rick hadn't washed the dishes, it would have been a mess. If Susie wasn't playing her role, the whole affair could have come crashing down in disorganization. But as each of these various people (and many others) exercised their individual gifts, a larger, beautiful gift came to be—a warm expression of the hospitality of our congregation toward our bishop.

If you're not using your gift for the building up of the body of Christ, well, that's really hard on the body. It is missing something because of that—not thriving as it could. You're valuable. In fact, God's Word says you're indispensable. When you use your gift, the Father is glorified and Jesus' body on earth thrives. But when you stay on the sidelines, the whole body is impaired.

YOU'RE VALUABLE.
IN FACT,
GOD'S WORD
SAYS YOU'RE
INDISPENSABLE.

REFLECT:

What is your gift and role in the body of Christ? How are you exercising it? Are you trying to exercise a gift or role in the body that truly is someone else's? Or are you on the sidelines, not knowing how you fit in? Ask your pastor and other believers to help you identify your personal gift, and then start using it so the whole congregation can thrive!

DAY 26
THURSDAY
THE GIFTS ARE TO BE USED TOGETHER
READ 1 CORINTHIANS 14:1-5

Some of the gifts of the Holy Spirit are designed to be used together. The *discernment of spirits* and *healing* is a good example.

Jesus rebuked and cast out many demons. Demons are real. But Jesus also healed medical conditions, such as the woman with a continual hemorrhage. Jesus was able to discern the true need of hurting individuals because He also had the gift of discernment of spirits.

None of us have all the gifts of the Holy Spirit, as Jesus did. That is why we need to work together, especially where some gifts are concerned. One of the important roles for someone with the gift of discernment of spirits is to help determine when someone is suffering from a medical condition versus being harmed by a demonic spirit.

It can be very hurtful if someone who is struggling with a medical condition is accused of being demonically possessed. I've seen this happen even within our own congregation when someone approached an individual who had a medical condition and accused the person of being demonically possessed. That's why someone with the gift of healing or the gift of casting out demons vitally needs someone with the gift of discernment of spirits to come alongside them to keep their gift in check.

In Jesus' day, it was believed that demons were the cause of many medical conditions, such as epilepsy. In our day and age, the opposite is true: we believe nothing is demon possession and everything is sickness! Both errors are equally destructive and dangerous.

That's why the gift of discernment of spirits is critically important today. As the Church, we need to be able to discern the error of our times—diagnosing everything as a medical problem when there is often spiritual oppression involved in the lives of people who are suffering. We often treat spiritual oppression with drugs when what the individual truly needs is prayer and inner healing or something else of a spiritual nature.

When an individual with the discernment of spirits recognizes a spiritual condition, it helps the person with the gift of healing to know how to effectively exercise his or her gift. In the same way, the person with the gift of healing completes the work of the gift of discernment. How helpful would it be if someone discerned spiritual oppression, but there was no one with the gift of healing prayer to do anything about it? These gifts need each other. They operate in partnership.

Another role for the gift of discernment of spirits is to separate true prophecy from false. The prophetic gift is one that needs other gifts to keep it in check. Somebody who speaks a word of knowledge saying, "This is what I hear the Lord speaking through me, for you," needs someone to come alongside who can test that prophecy. Paul gives an example in 1 Corinthians 14 when he encourages them to *"let two or three prophets speak, and let the others weigh what is said"* (1 Corinthians 14:29).

Satan can speak prophetically too. One of his most effective tactics is to use the Word of God inappropriately by misapplying it. Satan knows his Bible as well as any of us. There is an important role for the gift of discernment in determining if a prophecy is really from God or if it is of Satan. There are people who have this gift; not everyone does, but those who do are much needed in today's Church.

Just as the gift of discernment of spirits keeps in check the gifts of prophecy, healing, and casting out demons, other gifts are meant to work in union as well. For example, *speaking in tongues* is kept in check and elucidated by the *interpretation* of tongues. Paul says that if you don't have an interpreter, you shouldn't speak in tongues publicly. It doesn't show God's power. It builds one's self up rather than the body of Christ since what is spoken is unintelligible to others.

Now Paul isn't saying that speaking in tongues is bad. He actually says, *"I wish that you all spoke in tongues"* (1 Corinthians 14:5, NASB). He is being magnanimous, saying essentially, *I love speaking in tongues, you know. I speak in tongues more than any of you guys. I think it's great. But if you don't have an interpretation, it's worthless to the body, so you're just praying to God alone at that point. It's not a bad thing to do—pray to God alone in tongues, but it should be done privately at home.* When we exercise any of the gifts, we have to remember their purpose. The purpose of the public speaking of tongues is for the message to be interpreted so that it can encourage the whole congregation. You've got to have both gifts operating together—speaking and interpreting— in order for this gift to edify the body of Christ.

There are many more examples. All of the gifts benefit from the gift of *administration* being active in the Church. *Hospitality* is powerful when coupled with the gift of *teaching*, such as when someone opens their home to invite others to hear the teaching of the Scriptures.

Many gifts are designed to be used together, but the purpose of every gift is to build up the body, not ourselves. Sometimes really

gifted people, especially gifted preachers, teachers, and healers become so valued and prized for their gifts that they exercise them
in isolation, away from the rest of the body of Christ. This is dangerous. The Christian life is meant to be lived in community, not
alone. One of the reasons is so that our gifts can check each other's.
That's also why we dare not hold back our gifts. I may have certain
gifts, but if I don't have the other gifts keeping me in check, I get
off target. The same is true for you and the rest of those in your
congregation.

So don't hold back your gift. And if you have the gift of
encouragement, call out the spiritual gifts in the body and help
your fellow members see their importance and value. We all need
a little bit of encouragement!

THE CHRISTIAN LIFE IS MEANT TO BE
LIVED IN COMMUNITY, NOT ALONE.

REFLECT:

The idea of spiritual gifts functioning best together may be a new one. When have you seen gifts working together in a powerful way? When have you seen a gift used in isolation in a way that was damaging? How could your spiritual gift work well joined with another?

_____

_____

_____

_____

_____

_____

_____

_____

_____

_____

DAY 27
FRIDAY
DISCERN THE GIFTS
READ MATTHEW 7:7-11

How do you receive spiritual gifts? Or how do you discern those you already have?

The Apostle Paul challenges us to eagerly desire the gifts. So if you don't have a certain gift and would like to have it, ask God for it. They are gifts, so they are given. Jesus taught, *"Ask and it will be given to you."* He explained, *"Which of you, if your son asks for bread, will give him a stone? Or if he asks for a fish, will give him a snake? If you, then, though you are evil, know how to give good gifts to your children, how much more will your Father in heaven give good gifts to those who ask him!"* (Matthew 7:7, 9-11, NIV).

If your daughter asks you for a glass of water, you're not going to give her a scorpion. If your son asks for a sandwich, you're not going to give him a rat. The point is, if we as flawed human parents know how to give beneficial gifts to our children (often the ones they ask for), how much more does an all-knowing, all-loving Heavenly Father enjoy giving us good gifts?

But what are the gifts that the Father delights to give us?

Luke's Gospel says, *"how much more will your Father in heaven give the Holy Spirit to those who ask him!"* (Luke 11:13b, NIV).

So God wants to give us gifts—especially the Holy Spirit and the spiritual gifts that flow from Him. And Jesus wants to see those gifts manifested in the Church—His body on earth. So then, ask for gifts.

I've known people who really wanted to speak in tongues. I've never had a strong desire for that gift, but many people do. These individuals kept praying and asking God for that gift, and sure enough, God was pleased to give it to them. I know others who desired to be involved in a healing ministry. They prayed for the gift to be able to pray for people and see them healed, and I've watched God empower them to do that. Paul says, *"earnestly desire the spiritual gifts"* (1 Corinthians 14:1). So if there's something that is placed on your heart, it may be evidence that God longs to give you that gift. Simply ask for it.

But why do we have to ask? Why doesn't God just give us the gifts He wants us to have?

Sometimes God does just give gifts, but at other times I believe He wants us to show Him our desire by asking. Jesus says, *"Ask and it shall be given to you."* Remember the parable of the persistent widow? She asked and asked and asked for what she wanted. And finally, it was granted. Don't assume one little ask will get you the gift you want. Sometimes you've got to be persistent!

Besides asking for spiritual gifts, take some time to try to discern what gifts you may already have. How can you do that? First, if you think you have a particular gift, practice it and see what happens.

I've had people in my congregation tell me they have the gift of teaching. I say, "Okay, let's try it out." Sure enough, with some of these folks, they get up to teach and I think, "Wow, they are great teachers! Who knew?" Other times, it takes a while for a gift to develop. The gift I admired and desired from a young age was that of preaching and teaching. The first time I preached, it was pretty bad. It was horrible actually. I remember Father Don, my priest mentor, saying afterward, "That was what we call a 'take off and landing' sermon. You're coming in for a landing and then you just take back off again!" Yet he encouraged me to keep at it. You may not know you have a gift until you try it out. Even then, the effectiveness of your gift will improve with practice.

A second way to discern your gifts is to take a spiritual gifts inventory. These can be found online or through your pastor. Such evaluations can be helpful in identifying the different kinds of gifts and discovering the ones you gravitate toward.

Third, I like to ask people this question: "Where do you experience the presence of the Holy Spirit when you are involved in ministry?" This is an important question because you can feel the presence of God bubbling up within you when you are doing what God's gifted you to do! In the 1981 movie *Chariots of Fire*, the main character, Eric Liddell, has the gift of athleticism. He says, "I believe God made me for a purpose, but He also made me fast. And when I run, I feel His pleasure." [1]

God gives many kinds of gifts—physical, intellectual, emotional, spiritual. When we exercise any of those gifts for His glory, we feel fulfillment. But when we exercise a spiritual gift given to us for the benefit of the body of Christ, we experience a powerful sense of the Holy Spirit. The times I feel most spiritually connected to God are when I'm teaching and preaching. That's when I feel God working in my life and I know that's what I'm supposed to be doing. God provides internal confirmation of a spiritual gift when we sense His delight at its exercise. Interestingly, the opposite is also true. If someone tells me they don't feel very close to God or sense His presence, I often ask, "What are you doing for God right now?" If you're sitting on your gift, that's a very good reason why you might feel cold in your spirit.

Finally, our spiritual gifts are confirmed externally by the body of Christ. If gifts are given for the building up of the body, then their exercise will delight other believers. So when someone in the Church says to you, "Wow, when you did that (ministry/action), I really was blessed by God," that is a confirmation of a spiritual gift you've been given. Pay attention!

One day, I witnessed one of the members of our congregation be sworn in as the newly elected mayor of our town. A roomful of about 25 people was gathered in his support. I watched as David went around the room and identified each person by name, expressing why each one was special to him and how much it meant to him that they had come. My jaw dropped. I thought to myself, he has the spiritual gift of encouragement! I could see it so clearly as he used it to bless others. My role was to tell David what I saw in him and name the gift! As the pastor, I should be looking for ways to help him use that gift to bless the body.

When people say, "That blessed me," take note of it. And in turn, give confirmation to others when

WHEN WE EXERCISE A SPIRITUAL GIFT GIVEN TO US FOR THE BENEFIT OF THE BODY OF CHRIST, WE EXPERIENCE A POWERFUL SENSE OF THE HOLY SPIRIT.

you experience their gifts in action. If you've ever had a person pray aloud for you and felt like you'd been ushered directly to the throne of God, he or she has the gift of intercession. Tell them! Sometimes people do not even realize how they are blessing people and the impact God is having through their gifts unless someone tells them.

REFLECT:

When have you experienced internal confirmation of a gift of the Holy Spirit in your life? Where have you received external confirmation of a gift? I encourage you to be in a continual process of discerning what unique gifts the Lord has given you. And then, don't supress those gifts! Get busy using them. You will experience the amazing joy of God's presence as you do.

_____

_____

_____

_____

_____

_____

_____

_____

_____

DAY 28
SATURDAY
FROM GIFT TO GIFTED MINISTRY
READ EPHESIANS 4:11-16

There are many lists of spiritual gifts in the Bible, and there is overlap between them.

Some gifts are mentioned in two or more lists, others only once. There are gifts that may not be listed at all. Intercessory prayer is not listed in the Bible as a spiritual gift, yet it is certainly manifested in the Church. The point is, no individual list in Scripture contains all the gifts that may possibly be given to the people of God. Each list should be imagined to end with "etc."

As we study the lists, we see another distinction. In several lists, gifts are described as functions, such as prophecy, administration, teaching, discernment of spirits, etc. However, in Ephesians 4, the gifts are described as leadership roles, such as pastors, teachers, evangelists, prophets, and so forth.

The Apostle Paul puts it this way:

The gifts he gave were that some would be apostles, some prophets, some evangelists, some pastors and teachers, to equip the saints for the work of ministry, for building up the body of Christ, until all of us come to the unity of the faith and of the knowledge of the Son of God, to maturity, to the measure of the full stature of Christ.
Ephesians 4:11-13 (NRSV)

Sometimes a spiritual gift may manifest only for a particular moment as needed by the Holy Spirit. For example, I've prayed for people for healing and they've been healed, but I have not discerned that I have an ongoing gift of healing or an anointed ministry of healing. But sometimes, a spiritual gift becomes a ministry, which may become an anointed vocation.

For example, Judith and Frances McNutt have actually been anointed as healers in the life of the body of Christ, and they are widely recognized as such. For them, the gift of healing prayer became a vocation. When the body recognizes a particular prominence of a spiritual gift in a person, that person may be recognized, ordained, licensed, and anointed for a vocation using that gift.

The way the Church down through the ages has tried to differentiate people who have an office of ministry from those who use their gifts as laypersons is through terms like ordination. We say someone has been ordained as a pastor or ordained as an evangelist. We might use the term licensed. These terms indicate that such individuals are officially recognized by the larger body of Christ as set apart for a particular, ongoing ministry they have been called by God to carry out.

In the Episcopalian denomination, not only do we have the three ordained offices of bishop, priest, and deacon, but there also are several licensed lay ministries that are officially recognized, such as Eucharistic minister, Eucharistic visitors, catechist, pastoral leader, worship leader, and lay preacher. These roles may or may not be compensated financially by the Church. The key is to understand that God is continually raising up people for a variety of leadership positions in the Church. They are all desperately needed for the building up of the body.

What Paul is saying is that we need to be on the lookout for these individuals. We need to find ways to recognize and affirm those who have special gifts for ordained offices and licensed appointments and give them those roles in the body so that they will use those gifts vocationally.

For most members of the Church, a spiritual gift will remain an important lay ministry that needs to be part of the common life that the Lord has given the local congregation. (Sometimes people feel the empowering of the Spirit for ministry and mistake it for a call to the ordained ministry.) Nevertheless, the exercise of spiritual gifts in a lay capacity remains vitally important to the building up of the body. Just ask yourself how many times you've been blessed by the prayers, hospitality, mercy, teaching, or giving of someone who is not an ordained minister—probably more times than by those who hold ministry offices!

The key is to use your spiritual gifts in the context of your local congregation so that you can test and exercise your gifts. The body of Christ will be blessed and you can be encouraged to continue using your gifts. You may discover that God uses your gift as a blessing to others on particular occasions. Or you may discern, with the help of the body, that you have been specially gifted for an ongoing lay ministry or even an ordained office in the life of the Church. The Lord guides the Church in recognizing and calling forth the next generation of leaders.

One final thing to remember about a spiritual gift is that it's not about you.

Paul writes, *"For by the grace given to me I say to everyone among you not to think of yourself more highly than you ought to think, but to think with sober judgment, each according to the measure of faith that God has assigned"* (Romans 12:3, NRSV). And Peter says, *"If anyone speaks, they should do so as one who speaks the very words of God. If anyone serves, they should do so with the strength God provides, so that in all things God may be praised through Jesus Christ. To him be the glory and the power for ever and ever. Amen"* (1 Peter 4:11, NIV).

Use your gift not to build yourself up, but to build up the body of Christ. As good stewards of the manifold grace of God, we are called to serve others with whatever gift we have received and experience the amazing delight of God!

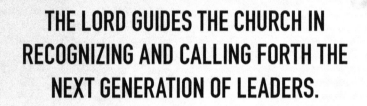

THE LORD GUIDES THE CHURCH IN RECOGNIZING AND CALLING FORTH THE NEXT GENERATION OF LEADERS.

REFLECT:

Pray and ask God to pour out on His Church the gifts of the Spirit. Pray that His people would discern their gifts and humbly use them so that the body can be fully what God is calling it to be— mature, strong, and healthy under Jesus Christ, to the praise of the Father.

_____

_____

_____

_____

_____

_____

_____

_____

_____

_____

EMPOWERED: THE WORK OF THE SPIRIT

So when [the disciples] had come together, they asked him, "Lord, will you at this time restore the kingdom to Israel?" He said to them, "It is not for you to know times or seasons that the Father has fixed by his own authority. But you will receive power when the Holy Spirit has come upon you, and you will be my witnesses in Jerusalem and in all Judea and Samaria, and to the end of the earth."

Acts 1:6-8

DAY 29
SUNDAY
THE LEVER OF GOD

READ EXODUS 31:1-4

Very early in the Bible, we learn about the nature and work of the Holy Spirit of God:

In the beginning, God created the heavens and the earth. The earth was without form and void, and darkness was over the face of the deep. And the Spirit of God was hovering over the face of the waters.   **Genesis 1:1-2**

God said, *"Let there be light"* (Genesis 1:3). Then He separated the light from the darkness and the sky from the deep. He created the land and animals, the birds and reptiles, the trees and creeping things—everything.

What we discover in Genesis 1:2 is that the Holy Spirit was present at Creation. He was the creative power of God. The Hebrew word for *spirit* is one of my favorite words in the Bible. It is *ruach*, and it's onomatopoetic, meaning that its sounds like what it means. If you say the word *ruach*, you hear the sound of your throat creating breath. And that's what *ruach* means—breath. The Holy Spirit is the breath of God.

Our English word *spirit* comes from the Latin word *spiritus*, which also means breath. You can see that the words *respiratory* and *expire* have roots in *spiritus*. Breath is the dynamic power of our lives. It is creative in the sense that it sustains our creation; it allows us to live. And so in Genesis 1, we find that the first mention of the Holy Spirit is as the *Holy Ruach*, the creative and life-giving breath of God.

The Holy Spirit is also present when God creates man: *"Then the Lord God formed the man of dust from the ground and breathed into his nostrils the breath of life, and the man became a living creature"* (Genesis 2:7). Where the text says, "the breath of life," it is the same Hebrew word, *ruach*. Anything that involves the flow of air—like wind, spirit, breath—are all the same word in Hebrew, *ruach*. The Holy Spirit gave *ruach*, breath, to man

So when we first meet the Holy Spirit in the Bible, we see two very powerful activities in which the Holy Spirit is involved: the Holy Spirit is dynamically involved in Creation, bringing order out of chaos, and the Holy Spirit is the agent who brings life, sending forth the very breath of life into human beings.

As we travel through the pages of the Scripture, we see that the Holy Spirit also is like the *lever* of God. One definition of the word *lever* is "an inducing or compelling force." The Holy Spirit is the active agent, the compelling force, who accomplishes the will of God in the world.

In the Old Testament, when God acts powerfully through a person, He always anoints that person with His Holy Spirit first. In today's reading from Exodus, we read that God filled Bezalel *"with the Spirit of God, with ability and intelligence, with knowledge and all craftsmanship, to devise artistic designs..."* (Exodus 31:1-4). And so, the Spirit is the One who gives this particular man (the chief artist for the temple) his incredible artistic ability and inspiration. In fact, the word *inspire* is another derivation of the word *spirit*. It literally means to "breathe into." We often speak of artists and musicians as being inspired—having been "breathed into" in a special way. Indeed, all godly creativity is an outworking of the creative power of the Holy Spirit who moved at the beginning of Creation.

There are many other examples of the Holy Spirit at work in the Old Testament. Samson is given incredible strength to break bonds and tear down buildings. It is the Holy Spirit who gave Samson that overpowering strength. Gideon is a reluctant and insecure man, chosen to lead the army of Israel. Gideon complained, *"Please, Lord, how can I save Israel? Behold, my clan is the weakest in Manasseh, and I am the least in my father's house"* (Judges 6:15). The Lord gives His Holy Spirit to empower Gideon with leadership abilities to live up to his name as a mighty man of valor. The source of Gideon's valor is not himself, but the Holy Spirit of God.

When the prophets of God speak the words of God, it's always the Holy Spirit empowering them to speak. When God anoints prophets, priests, and kings to lead Israel, it's always the anointing of the Holy Spirit that comes upon and enables these leaders.

When God wants to work powerfully in a person's life or do a mighty act in nature, such as parting the Red Sea by a mighty rushing wind or raising to life the dry bones in Ezekiel, The Holy Spirit is the One—the person of God—who actually accomplishes these powerful and mighty acts. By the operation of the Spirit, worlds are created, dead bones live, enemies are vanquished, and souls are saved.

The lever of God. When you place a lever under something, it is pried free. Heavy objects are moved, weights are lifted, and freedom of movement is possible. That is the Lord's work in our lives, from Creation through Redemption to Salvation, all through His lever—the Holy Spirit.

The Holy Spirit is the power that can liberate you. The Spirit can break any bondage or weight that ties you down. The Spirit can convert your heart, change your life, and vanquish your enemies—including your greatest enemy, death itself. Our human problem is that we have no real grasp of the immense power of God in the Spirit.

This is why the Apostle Paul prays for the Church, that the eyes of our hearts would be opened to see and believe in the power of God's Spirit. Why? So that we may know:

"...what is the immeasurable greatness of his power toward us who believe, according to the working of his great might that he worked in Christ when he raised him from the dead and seated him at his right hand in the heavenly places, far above all rule and authority and power and dominion, and above every name that is named, not only in this age but also in the one to come."
Ephesians 1:19-21

THE SPIRIT CAN BREAK ANY BONDAGE OR WEIGHT THAT TIES YOU DOWN.

Paul would go on to pray that the people of God would *"be strengthened with power through his Spirit"* in their inner being to the glory of *"him who is able to do far more abundantly than all that we ask or think, according to the power at work within us"* (Ephesians 3:16, 20).

The power of the Holy Spirit of God is immeasurably great! It is the very power that raised Jesus Christ from the dead and exalted Him above every rule and authority. That same power is within you. As a baptized, adopted, transformed, and equipped Spirit-filled Christian, the lever of God is at work in you and through you!

REFLECT:

When have you seen the Holy Spirit work in power? What was that experience like? Do you ever doubt that the same power that raised Christ from the dead is at work in you, and available to you as you minister to others? If so, ask God to "open the eyes of your heart" to see and believe in the power of God's lever, the Holy Spirit.

_____

_____

_____

_____

_____

_____

_____

_____

_____

_____

DAY 30
MONDAY
TREASURE IN JARS OF CLAY
READ 2 CORINTHIANS 4:7-18

Yesterday we talked about the immeasurable power of God's Holy Spirit. Today we are going to talk about the contrast to that power—our human weakness.

In the beloved children's song, "Jesus Loves Me," there is a line that says, "They are weak, but He is strong." It's talking about children, but the truth is, we are all weak in our human flesh, not just "little ones," but all of us. We need the power of God operating in us because we have no strength without it. The Scriptures say, *"In him we live and move and have our being"* (Acts 17:28). That means that no human being would even exist without God's sustaining power!

Fundamental to understanding the Christian life is grasping hold of the paradox of our weakness in the flesh and God's power within us, in the Spirit. For this is precisely the way the apostle Paul talks about the work of the Holy Spirit:

But we have this treasure in jars of clay, to show that the surpassing power belongs to God and not to us. We are afflicted in every way, but not crushed; perplexed, but not driven to despair; persecuted, but not forsaken; struck down, but not destroyed; always carrying in the body the death of Jesus, so that the life of Jesus may also be manifested in our bodies.   **2 Corinthians 4:7-10**

Our physical bodies are compared to jars of clay. What do you think of when you think of a jar of clay? Brittle. Easily cracked. Breaks when it falls. Throw a rock at it and it shatters. It's vulnerable to be a jar of clay! Yet the Apostle Paul has in mind more than just our physical bodies; he is speaking of who we are in our entirety. (Note that when Paul talks about being "perplexed," he is referring to psychological frailty.)As human beings, we are jars of clay—finite, weak, and fragile—in every aspect of our beings— physically, mentally, emotionally, and spiritually.

But within that jar of clay is something of incredible power and strength! That is the Spirit of God. We weak vessels—jars of clay— possess within us a surpassing power that is not ours, but of God's.

Human weakness comes in so many forms. We are weak in the face of the general suffering and pain that characterizes this age. We are weak when assaulted by what are sometimes call non-moral evil: sickness, poverty, and calamities that happen in this world. We are vulnerable to the moral evils of persecution and injustice from sinful people and violent acts. Our minds can become sick with depression, anxiety, and despair.

Paul knows such weaknesses personally. But in the midst of Paul's suffering, God encourages him:

But [the Lord] said to me, "My grace is sufficient for you, for my power is made perfect in weakness." Therefore I will boast all the more gladly of my weaknesses, so that the power of Christ may rest upon me. For the sake of Christ, then, I am content with weaknesses, insults, hardships, persecutions, and calamities. For when I am weak, then I am strong.   **2 Corinthians 12:9-10**

Would the people of this world make a statement like that? "When I'm weak, then I am strong!" I don't think so! This world values the strong—physically, intellectually, emotionally, and financially. We want to have big muscles, look handsome, be smart, and have people look up to us. Power, with respect to the world, means having lots of money, enjoying the security of position and prestige, and demonstrating control and authority. So we want lifts and tucks, awards and accolades, promotions and raises—the things that will make us bigger and greater in the world's eyes.

But Paul is saying quite the opposite. He is embracing all the weak things about himself. He is not boasting about prestige among men or spiritual position. (Paul was both well-educated and called as an apostle). Rather, he boasts in his insecurities—weaknesses, insults, hardships, persecutions. A bad reputation is an insult. Financial tribulation is a hardship.

The context of these statements is Paul's plea to God to remove a chronic personal weakness from him: a thorn in the flesh that he asks God to take from him multiple times. But the Lord says no.

So to keep me from becoming conceited because of the surpassing greatness of the revelations, a thorn was given me in the flesh, a messenger of Satan to harass me, to keep me from becoming conceited. Three times I pleaded with the Lord about this, that it should leave me. But he said to me, "My grace is sufficient for you..."
2 Corinthians 12:7-9

Have you ever thought about what that "thorn in the flesh" might have been for Paul? It's a common phrase that people still use today. Sometimes people will say of an annoying person: "He's a thorn in my side!" But what was it for Paul? *What was his thorn?* We know Paul was once physically blinded (Acts 9:9), and was shipwrecked and beaten. Perhaps it was poor eyesight or some other injury that would not heal. It could have been something spiritual—a temptation that Satan continually put before him. From his letter to the Romans, we know Paul struggled with covetousness (Romans 7:7-25). Perhaps Paul was being tormented by Satan, the accuser of the brethren. Paul was a past persecutor of Christians and complicit in the murder of Stephen. Maybe he was constantly hearing, "You're a failure, you're a fake; look how you stood by while they stoned Stephen!" Paul knew he was not that guy anymore, but maybe that recording kept playing in his mind.

For some reason, the apostle was vague about the nature of his thorn in the flesh. What is clear is that it was a chronic personal challenge that he saw as Satan's opportunity to "harass" him continually.

We all can relate to Paul, as we all have weaknesses and challenges. We pray the same prayers, "Lord, take this away!" And yet, often it remains. The overarching point is that these kinds of obstacles are part of living in a fallen world, and we all have them.

Having a chronic weakness makes us humble. It causes us to rely on the Lord's strength more fully. God wants you to depend on Him—always.

And most wonderful of all, a thorn in the flesh is an opportunity for the power of God to really show forth in your life! When you have a chronic weakness, God does something amazing

IN THE PLACES OF GREATEST WEAKNESS FOR YOU, THE STRENGTH OF THE SPIRIT RADIATES MOST GLORIOUSLY.

in spite of that weakness—He makes His glory shine more abundantly through it! In the places of greatest weakness for you, the strength of the Spirit radiates most gloriously.

Nothing is stronger than God in you. The treasure you hold in a fragile jar of clay is the all-surpassing power of the Spirit of God!

REFLECT:

A thorn in the flesh could be anything with which you are personally and perpetually struggling. What is your thorn in the flesh?
Hear the promise from God to you, "My grace is sufficient for you,
for my power is made perfect in weakness." Accept that you are
a jar of clay, but know that the immeasurable power of the Holy
Spirit is in you and empowers you!

_____

_____

_____

_____

_____

_____

_____

_____

_____

_____

DAY 31
TUESDAY
THE LIE OF THE WORLD
READ 1 CORINTHIANS 2:1-5

The lie of the world is that we need to be strong in our own humanity.

God says just the opposite. He says, "I want to be your strength. I want to be your power. You don't need to be strong according to the flesh. When you are weak, then you are strong in me." That's the idea.

When we humble ourselves, we admit our weaknesses, acknowledge our struggles, and allow God's power to come in. That's when we are transformed. That is how God is glorified in and through us.

It takes a lot of courage to ask someone for help—particularly when it is a personal, private struggle. One of my parishioners named James asked that my wife, Brooke, and I pray for him together. There weren't a lot of specifics about what he needed; he just humbled himself to ask. So my very discerning wife suggested that we spend a couple of minutes quietly praying and asking the Holy Spirit how to use the time.

As I was praying, I started to feel a painful knot in my stomach. I never have stomach pains. At first I kept the feelings to myself, but the pain would not go away! I very clearly heard the Lord saying,

"Pray for James' stomach." So I said, "This may sound silly, but I really feel like we need to pray for James' stomach."

He said, "Yes, that's it!"

Unbeknownst to us, James had stored all his worry, stress, and anxiety in his gut. It actually caused him tremendous pain and physical problems. But the root of it all was fear about his career, which was very uncertain, and about his marriage, which was in a turbulent place.

As we prayed for James and his stomach, we also lifted up all the anxieties he had verbalized. The promise of the Holy Spirit came upon him. James was given *"the peace of God, which surpasses all understanding"* (Philippians 4:7).

I marvel at the power of the Lord. We could have spent an hour talking and digging into James' personal life to try to draw out his specific needs. But in a matter of two prayerful minutes, the Holy Spirit revealed how we should pray, and God's power was displayed mightily in another person's life! In our weakness, God was strong.

That's what intercessory prayer can do. It acknowledges the reality of another person's pain before God. It's not rocket science, by the way. Anyone can do it. My wife and I simply took the hurts and worries of another person to the Lord by first listening and then repeating what James said to God. When we all needed clarity, we asked the Holy Spirit to help. God revealed James' exact struggle to me in a way I could empathize with (stomach pains). Together, we prayed about James' hardships. We were vulnerable together in the weakness of the flesh that we all share, and we stood in that place as fellow believers.

Are we willing to accept weakness in others? Are we willing to be humble and acknowledge our own weaknesses?

The challenge of vulnerability is to take down the masks, to remove the facade, and to disassemble the walls we've erected. That's how we allow God to unleash His awesome power and work in our lives.

So often we compare our inner self to another person's outer self. We wrongly believe that we have to show the appearance of strength to others. We try to hide our insecurities, embarrassments, and vulnerabilities. These are the things that cause us shame, so we tuck them away. When we hide, we don't let God's light shine in, and we do not get healing. Our weaknesses become a place of defeat.

But there's another way. The grace of God and our confidence in the Spirit of God within us allows us to come out of hiding and be vulnerable. Such confidence in the Spirit gives us freedom to minister to others from the place of our own weakness. This is the powerful message of Henri Nouwen's classic book *The Wounded Healer*—that our human weakness is actually what gives us the strength and ability to minister to others, through empathy. [1]

Empathy is critically important for human relationships. One of the reasons why shame is such a powerful force in so many people's lives is that nobody draws alongside them, empathizing with them and saying, "I hear that struggle, and I feel that with you." Empathy doesn't judge; it acknowledges and shares the other's struggle.

That is not to say that we don't hope and pray for victory, renewal, and change in another's life. My wife and I advocated in prayer for James to see light and life. But what James needed was not words of wisdom from me—he needed to be ushered into the presence of the Prince of Peace. The Spirit brings life. I can only seek the Spirit with him.

In and of myself, I can't fix another person. I can't even fix myself! But as Christians, we know who can fix it all. We know and believe in God— the Creator, Redeemer, and Sustainer of all life who, through His Holy Spirit, unleashes great power to help and to heal. We offer this power of the Spirit to those who are struggling, just as one beggar graciously shows another where to find bread. We are to draw alongside the weak in our weakness and let God's power do the heavy lifting.

We are to serve as Paul served:

And I was with you in weakness and in fear and much trembling, and my speech and my message were not in plausible words of wisdom, but in demonstration of the Spirit and of power, so that your faith might not rest in the wisdom of men but in the power of God.
1 Corinthians 2:3-5

Jesus' body was crucified in weakness, but He lived anew in the power of God and the power of the Holy Spirit. Likewise, in your weakness, you share in the sufferings of Christ, but also experience the power of His Resurrection. The self-denial of the Crucified Life and the new birth of the Resurrected Life culminate in the Spirit-filled Life—a life in which, though we are weak according to the flesh, we are powerful because of God's Spirit's working in us and through us!

EMPATHY IS CRITICALLY
IMPORTANT FOR HUMAN
RELATIONSHIPS.

REFLECT:

God will use you to do amazing things! Be with others in their weakness in order that the grace of God might shine through you. Rely on the Spirit to give you the right words to say, or show you when to listen reflectively. Your own vulnerability and empathy will enable you to be a vessel of God's grace to others.

_____

_____

_____

_____

_____

_____

_____

_____

_____

_____

DAY 32
WEDNESDAY
THE GATES OF HELL
READ MATTHEW 16:13-19

The key turning point in the three synoptic Gospels (Matthew, Mark, and Luke) [2] often is identified as "the confession of St. Peter." From this point on, it is clear that the disciples know who Jesus is; the focus now shifts to revealing what Jesus came to do—to defeat the very forces of death and hell through the sacrifice of His life and His victory over the grave.

Let's take a closer look at this confession of St. Peter:

Now when Jesus came into the district of Caesarea Philippi, he asked his disciples, "Who do people say that the Son of Man is?" And they said, "Some say John the Baptist, others say Elijah, and others Jeremiah or one of the prophets." He said to them, "But who do you say that I am?" Simon Peter replied, "You are the Christ, the Son of the living God."   **Matthew 16:13-16**

Peter is the one who spoke up. He spoke with confidence and passion: *"You are the Christ, the Son of the living God"* (Matthew 16:16). Here we get an inkling that Jesus wants to do some amazing things through Simon Peter after his faith-filled confession:

Jesus answered him, "Blessed are you, Simon Bar-Jonah! For flesh and blood has not revealed this to you, but my Father who is in

heaven. And I tell you, you are Peter, and on this rock I will build my Church, and the gates of hell shall not prevail against it."
Matthew 16:17-18

Sometimes when this passage is taught, the Church is pictured as a fort under attack by Satan. We're on the defense, standing our ground. The Scriptures do tell us to stand our ground against the devil (Ephesians 6). But this mindset of hunkering down and pro-tecting ourselves from the evil one is not what Jesus is teaching.

In Caesarea Philippi, where this exchange takes place, there was a cave called the Grotto of Pan where people worshiped a very evil little demon. He was half-goat, half-man, and played a pipe. The people believed Pan's Grotto was an entrance to the nether-world—the gates of hell.

So when Jesus mentions "the gates of hell," He is saying that, though de-mons may have their fortresses set up in Caesarea Philippi and other places around the world, you, Peter, and the other disciples are now on the *offensive*. Satan's fortresses will not stand against you! The Church is on the march.

The mission of the Church is not *defensive*—to self-protect from evil by gathering into holy huddles. Rather, its mission is to go forth on the *offense*, tearing down strongholds of the evil one in people's lives and in communities around this world.

The Church carries out this mission under a new cosmology. Let me explain. During the time before Christ, the only place where God exercised His reign on earth was in Israel. The Lord's capital city was Jerusalem, and the Temple was where the footstool of God's throne resided. So if you wanted to be, in a sense, within the Kingdom of God, you needed to go to Jerusalem and be among the people of Israel. The cities and nations of the Gentile world, such as Caesarea Philippi, were all under the dominion of false gods and the evil one.

But with the death and Resurrection of Jesus, everything changed! The fabric of power and authority in the cosmos shifted. A new sheriff had come to town. His name was Jesus. *"All authority in heaven and on earth has been given to me,"* says Jesus. *"Go therefore and make disciples of all nations..."* (Matthew 28:18-19).

And it's not just this world that is gradually changing hands. Paul teaches that, through the Church, by the administration of the Gospel, *"the manifold wisdom of God might now be made known to the rulers and authorities in the heavenly places"* (Ephesians 3:10). Through the power of the Gospel, the demonic forces of evil in the heavenly realms are put on notice that they are no longer in charge of this world or any other! All cities, towns, and people in the entire world who lived under Satan's dominion will soon bow to the Lordship of Christ.

This transition is a gradual process. It will not be complete until Jesus comes again in power on the last day when *"every knee will bow... and every tongue will confess that Jesus Christ is Lord, to the glory of God the Father"* (Philippians 2:10-11, NASB). Until that day, we Christians are to go forth in the power of God, taking down strongholds of the evil one and bringing the hope and freedom of Jesus Christ to this world. There is no place on this earth where Satan's strongholds are safe from the power of the Spirit of Christ. We are to clean up the global mess that has been Satan's playground for far too long!

So many Christians in the developed world see the Church as a place to go and hear a compelling sermon on a Sunday morning, to be inspired and even entertained. Instead, Sunday morning is to be the time we regroup and hear our marching orders for the coming week's battles. The famous preacher Charles Spurgeon put it this way:

> *Churches are not made that men of ready speech may stand up on Sundays and talk, and so win daily bread from their admirers. No, there is another end and aim for this. These places of worship are not built that you may sit comfortably and hear something that shall make you pass away your Sundays with pleasure.*
>
> *A Church which does not exist to do good in the slums, and dens, and kennels of the city, is a Church that has no reason to justify its longer existing. A Church that does not exist to reclaim heathenism, to fight with evil, to destroy error, to put down falsehood, a Church that does not exist to take the side of the poor, to denounce injustice and to hold up righteousness, is a Church that has no right to be.*
>
> *Not for yourself, O Church, do you exist, any more than Christ existed for Himself. His glory was that He laid aside His glory, and the glory of the Church is when she lays aside her respectability and her dignity, and counts it to be her glory to gather together the outcasts, and her highest honor to seek amid the foulest mire the priceless jewels for which Jesus shed His blood. To rescue souls from hell and lead to God, to hope, to heaven, this is her heavenly occupation. O that the Church would always feel this!* [3]

Jesus taught His disciples to pray to the Father a very powerful prayer:

"Your kingdom come, your will be done, on earth as it is in heaven."
Matthew 6:10

Whenever Jesus entered a gathering of people, He would announce, *"The kingdom of God is at hand"* (Mark 1:15, Matthew 3:2, 4:17). When the President of the United States walks in, the band strikes up "Hail to the Chief." Whenever Jesus walks into the room, the choirs of heaven sing a greater song:

> *All hail the pow'r of Jesus' Name!*
> *Let angels prostrate fall;*
> *Bring forth the royal diadem,*
> *And crown Him Lord of all!*
>
> *Let every kindred, every tribe,*
> *On this terrestrial ball,*
> *To Him all majesty ascribe,*
> *And crown Him Lord of all!* [4]

Where the Church is, the King is present in the power of the Holy Spirit. Knees bend and hearts fall to the obedience of faith in Jesus Christ. The power of God is mightily at work in and through you, as the Church marches forward, unseating all powers, authorities, and principalities that are ruling over the people of this world. *The gates of hell will not stand against it!*

REFLECT:

Do you see Sunday morning more as a time to hear a nice sermon or a time to receive your "marching orders" for the week? Have you ever seen the Church move in power against the strongholds of Satan? How so? Pray that God will empower His Church to go on the offensive in your community, and empower you personally to march where He calls.

DAY 33
THURSDAY
THE BATTLEFIELD OF THE MIND

READ 2 CORINTHIANS 10:1-5

Paul taught over and over again that Christians are not to walk according to the flesh. *According to the flesh* means indulging in sinful behavior.

But there is a difference between walking *in the flesh* and walking *according to the flesh*. Paul writes: *"For though we walk in the flesh, we are not waging war according to the flesh"* (2 Corinthians 10:3).

For Paul, strength was not found in his own human talents or strengths. Paul would exercise his authority, but not with human strength and human power. Some said of Paul that his *"bodily presence is weak"* and that his *"speech was of no account"* (2 Corinthians 10:10). Paul saw those fleshly limitations as advantages in the spiritual battle for the minds and hearts of men. He writes:

The weapons we fight with are not the weapons of the world. On the contrary, they have divine power to demolish strongholds. We demolish arguments and every pretension that sets itself up against the knowledge of God, and we take captive every thought to make it obedient to Christ.   **2 Corinthians 10:4-5 (NIV)**

Beloved of God, know that we are in a battle, but the battle is not against flesh and blood (Ephesians 6:12), but against Satan and the spiritual forces of evil. However, Satan will use flesh and blood to wage war against us. This is what Paul means by "strongholds."

A spiritual stronghold is a base of operation from which Satan can wage war against the Kingdom of God and its people. These fortresses are created when a person falls prey to the devil's schemes and consequently provides Satan a foothold to erect a base within the battlefield of our minds.

Here is an example of how it works: Paul writes to the Church in Ephesus, *"'In your anger do not sin.' Do not let the sun go down while you are still angry, and do not give the devil a foothold"* (Ephesians 4:26-27, NIV). Anger is a typical human response to an offense or injury in this fallen world; yet, when nursed in the mind over time, anger can become a breeding ground for satanic activity. Satan can use the angry person to speak accusations, to cause fights, and even to do violence.

I've seen many marriages in which one spouse becomes the voice of satanic accusation against the other, ripping the beloved to shreds within the privacy and sacred space of the home. Satan is the accuser of the brothers and sisters of Christ (Revelation 12:10), not you! You are to speak the truth in love as the voice of maturity in the Lord.

Any capitulation to temptation can give rise to a satanic stronghold in a person's life: lust, malice, greed, doubt, envy, etc. When we fall prey to the devil, we can be used by him for evil. Our minds and hearts will be occupied either by the Holy Spirit of God or the forces of the evil one—there is no neutral ground in this war. *"Submit yourselves therefore to God. Resist the devil, and he will flee from you. Draw near to God, and he will draw near to you"* (James 4:7-8).

When we interview a baptismal candidate in our Church, we ask them if they will renounce Satan and the spiritual forces of evil that rebel against God. In this renunciation, the candidate is kicking Satan off the property! The newly-baptized Christian is planting his or her flag squarely in the Kingdom of God and taking sides in the war under the banner of Jesus Christ. But that doesn't mean that the war is over! Satan will continue to assault the new or re-committed believer because Satan hates losing a stronghold. He will marshal all of his forces to seek to reclaim lost ground to re-build his fortresses.

So long as you're here on this planet, even if you're a strong Christian, you are in the battle. The call is to live in the world, but not of it. Satanic power and strongholds will never be dislodged from their positions by human effort or strength. Those who rely on human powers in the battle only serve to strengthen the position of the evil one. We are in the flesh, but we do not wage war according to the flesh. Our weapons and armor are spiritual in nature, power, and strength.

Adopted child of God, the Holy Spirit is our power to stand firm against the devil in the midst of the fight. Until the Day of Resurrection, you are in the fight of your life. And the battlefield is your mind. Contend in your own human strength and not only will you lose, but you will become complicit with the enemy.

Rely on the Holy Spirit for strength, and you will not only defend against Satan, but also defeat him and his minions in the battlefield of your mind. As the Apostle John writes, *"Little children, you are from God and have overcome them, for he who is in you is greater than he who is in the world"* (1 John 4:4).

REFLECT:

Do you ever feel like you are losing the battle against Satan, that he is setting up a fortress in your mind or heart? Right now, cry out to God for help. Repent of allowing Satan a foothold and ask the Holy Spirit to tear down any stronghold of sin in your life—lust, anger, greed, unforgiveness. The Holy Spirit's power is immeasurably able to break those bonds and set you free right now!

_____

_____

_____

_____

_____

_____

_____

_____

_____

DAY 34
FRIDAY
YOU SHALL RECEIVE POWER

READ LUKE 4:31-37

Just before His Ascension to the right hand of the Father, Jesus said this to His disciples:

But you will receive power when the Holy Spirit has come upon you, and you will be my witnesses in Jerusalem and in all Judea and Samaria, and to the end of the earth.   **Acts 1:8**

Jesus taught that the Kingdom of God would begin to spread like waves from the epicenter of an earthquake. The movement would begin in the capital city of Jerusalem and then move into Judea, the geographic region around Jerusalem. Samaria would be the next wave, and then the Kingdom of God would ripple out to the ends of the earth.

A force more powerful than a nuclear explosion went forth on the day of Pentecost! With the outpouring of the Holy Spirit on the disciples gathered in Jerusalem, a force began to sweep across this planet more intense than any power it had seen before—a spiritual power capable of unseating thrones, powers, and the principalities of evil.

But even before Pentecost, when Jesus walked and taught on the earth, He was a man of authority and power. Every place He went,

Jesus manifested power. In Luke 4:31-36, we read how Jesus went into Capernaum, a city of Galilee, and taught the people. Luke writes, *"And they were astonished at his teaching, for his word possessed authority"* (Luke 4:32).

Whenever the King shows up, the prevailing powers are threatened—and they do not go down without a fight! When Jesus displayed His authority in Capernaum, a man with a demonic spirit confronted Him in an effort to reassert control of the synagogue and town. The demon arched up in the face of Jesus and said, *"Ha! What have you to do with us, Jesus of Nazareth? Have you come to destroy us? I know who you are—the Holy One of God"* (Luke 4:34).

This was a demonic military challenge. But with a simple command from Jesus, *"Be silent and come out of him!"* (Luke 4:35), the demon departed without another word.

The Lord simply says, "You're out," and removes the demonic stronghold with the power of the Word and Spirit. The people of the synagogue were amazed and marveled, *"What is this word? For with authority and power he commands the unclean spirits, and they come out!"* (Luke 4:36).

The man with the demon was liberated in that moment; he was free! And the crowd recognized it. But what else happened when that spiritual power went forth? The people in the town of Capernaum experienced physical healings: *"And all the crowd sought to touch him, for power came out from him and healed them all"* (Luke 6:19). As the power of God manifests spiritually, physical and emotional restorations take place—people are healed in various ways.

Lisa was the daughter of members of our Church and the young mother of two children. When I was called to the hospital, Lisa was in critical condition. Her colon had lost blood flow and had literally died. The doctors were about to attempt a very dangerous surgery. I was there to pray, and a lawyer was present to help her write her will!

Lisa's parents had alerted believers all over the country who were praying fervently for a miracle from God for her.

Because of the difficulty of the surgery and odds of even surviving (a 50-50 chance), only one surgeon was willing to take Lisa's case. Interestingly, his name was Dr. De Jesus. A group of medical interns would attend the surgery to learn how these difficult cases were handled.

The day before the dangerous surgery, a pre-operative colonoscopy was performed. As Dr. De Jesus, a second surgeon, and the interns examined the results, they stared in utter amazement. What they saw on the screens was a completely healed and perfectly healthy colon. Lisa's arteries and veins had reconnected, and her colon had regenerated.

The vascular surgeon exclaimed, "That is impossible! That can't happen!" At that moment, Dr. De Jesus turned and gave a lecture to the medical interns on the power and will of God to heal. He said, "The vascular surgeon says, 'That is impossible.' But sometimes God does the impossible. And there can be no other explanation." Amen!

In the New Testament, we see that the Lord's power on earth is revealed in a three-fold process. First, Jesus teaches with authority and power, proclaiming the Kingdom of God. Second, He removes demonic oppressors and unseats them from their places of power. Once the demonic forces are unseated, people are healed and restored. Third, Jesus distributes His power.

You'll see in Luke 9:1-2 that the first people to whom Jesus distributes his power are the twelve Apostles. He sends them out to proclaim the Kingdom of God. Through the Holy Spirit, He gives them authority over all demons as well as the power to cure diseases. Notice that this pattern is the same as that of Jesus: the Apostles first proclaim the Kingdom of God and unseat the spiritual forces of evil. That's when healings begin to take place.

Jesus then broadens the distribution of His power from the twelve to the seventy-two (Luke 10:17-20). When he sends these disciples out, they come back amazed, *"Lord, even the demons are subject to us in your name!"* Jesus replies that they don't know the half of it! *"I saw Satan fall like lightening from heaven"* (Luke 10:18). What He is saying is that, not only are we winning the ground war, but also the larger cosmic war (that you and I can't see). The evil one is being unseated—God's Kingdom is on the move!

This distribution of Jesus' power culminates with the outpouring of the Holy Spirit on Pentecost. *"You shall receive power to be my witnesses,"* He says to the gathered disciples. He is commissioning them to continue His work on earth through the Spirit's power. But this time it can go farther. In fact, Jesus says that it's better for Him to go to the Father: *"Truly, truly, I say to you, whoever believes in me will also do the works that I do; and greater works than these will he do, because I am going to the Father"* (John 14:12).

The Holy Spirit now can carry out Jesus' work in this world not just with twelve or seventy-two followers, but with multitudes. Seventy is about the limit of how many people one individual can administrate. As a pastor, I know it's hard to be in a personal relationship with many more people than seventy and do it well.

Jesus was limited in His human body; but when He ascends into the Heavenly realms, He can now be in a personal relationship (through the Holy Spirit) with conceivably every person on the planet.

So now Jesus is not sending out twelve or seventy; He's sending out millions in His power! That includes us. And what are we to do? We are to proclaim the Kingdom of God, unseat the powers of oppression and darkness, and heal and restore in His name. We do all this under the Holy Spirit's administration, whose purpose is to fulfill the plan of God to finally bring all things into submission under the One Lord, Jesus Christ:

With all wisdom and understanding, he made known to us the mystery of his will according to his good pleasure, which he purposed in Christ, to be put into effect when the times reach their fulfillment—to bring unity to all things in heaven and on earth under Christ. **Ephesians 1:8-10 (NIV)**

REFLECT:

Jesus first proclaims the Kingdom of God with authority and then unseats powers of evil and darkness. That is when healings take place. How can you, in the power of the Holy Spirit, proclaim the Kingdom where you are? How can you pray to unseat the powers of evil? Ask God to direct you, and you will see amazing displays of His power to heal and restore.

_____

_____

_____

_____

_____

_____

_____

_____

_____

_____

DAY 35
SATURDAY
SPIRITUAL WARFARE
READ EPHESIANS 6:10-20

I once went to the doctor with an injured knee only to find out that the root of the problem was not my knee, but my ankle, which had lost its mobility. When I rehabbed my ankle, the symptoms in my knee disappeared.

Far too often, we Christians fight the symptoms of sin rather than the real problem. We see the outworking of evil in the world in immorality, corruption, and even the violent persecution of the Church. But the teaching of Jesus and the Apostles is that the root problem of evil is spiritual in nature:

For our struggle is not against flesh and blood, but against the rulers, against the authorities, against the powers of this dark world and against the spiritual forces of evil in the heavenly realms.

Ephesians 6:12 (NIV)

Being empowered by the Holy Spirit is fundamentally about enlisting in the Lord's Army, joining Him in waging the ultimate war against Satan and the forces of evil. Sadly, all too many Christians live as if there is no war, oblivious to Satan's diabolical plans to *"steal, kill and destroy"* (John 10:10).

Which Army General wouldn't love to have his opponent underestimate him, or even ignore his existence altogether? This is precisely what much of the Church in the developed world does when it comes to spiritual warfare—underestimate Satan or just ignore him. Yet, the devil's schemes are perfected. (The developing world tends to take spiritual warfare more seriously.) You and I are called to take our stand against him and defeat him.

Satan's fundamental scheme is to have flesh and blood do battle against flesh and blood. But to approach the battle that way is to take up the very arms of Satan and adopt his tactics.

No, the people of God are called to fight with spiritual armor and spiritual weaponry. Then no power of hell can prevail! *"Therefore put on the full armor of God, so that when the day of evil comes, you may be able to stand your ground, and after you have done everything, to stand"* (Ephesians 6:13).

Notice the verse doesn't say *if* the day of evil comes, but *when*. It will come. All true Christians are called upon to be ready to contend with the forces of evil; so put on the full armor of God!

Ephesians 6 identifies six critical pieces of defensive armor:

Stand firm then, with the belt of truth buckled around your waist, with the breastplate of righteousness in place, and with your feet fitted with the readiness that comes from the gospel of peace. In addition to all this, take up the shield of faith, with which you can extinguish all the flaming arrows of the evil one. Take the helmet of salvation..." **Ephesians 6:14-17**

For a soldier, the *belt* holds everything together. The belt of God's armor is *Truth*. Why? Because, as Jesus describes, Satan is the chief deceiver: *"He was a murderer from the beginning, not holding to the truth, for there is no truth in him. When he lies, he speaks his native language, for he is a liar and the father of lies"* (John 8:44, NIV).

To wear the **Belt of Truth** means that, at the core of our beings, we are people of absolute truth. Jesus prayed to the Father on our behalf, *"Sanctify them in the truth; your word is truth"* (John 17:17). Our culture teaches that truth is relative; it is captive to the chief liar. How do we combat these lies? We read, mark, learn, and inwardly digest the Word of God—the Truth. How much time do you devote to studying the Bible, reading Christian books, and sitting under godly teachers? Buckle up!

The *breastplate* protects the soldier's most vital organ—the heart. One of Satan's tactics is to corrupt the heart with unrighteousness. Like a spear, the works of the flesh pierce the heart and take a godly man or woman down. We all know pillars of the Church who fell to the spears of unrighteousness by capitulating to ungodly temptations and hardness of heart. Every morning when you wake, prayerfully center your heart on the Lord. Worship Him weekly in corporate gatherings. Eliminate the sources of temptation on your computers and from your television, at your workplace and at home. Maintain accountable fellowship with zealous believers. A heart vulnerable to unrighteousness is an easy target for the evil one. Satan aims for your heart. So guard your heart every day by equipping yourself with the **Breastplate of Righteousness.**

Without proper *footwear*, a soldier cannot last long in the fight; he or she definitely cannot march to battle. We are instructed to have *"...shod your feet with the preparation of the gospel of peace"* (Ephesians 6:15, NKJV). This means that every Christian needs to be prepared to share the Gospel of peace that comes through knowing Jesus. Do you know how to share the hope you have in Jesus with an unbelieving co-worker, neighbor, or friend? The Lord wants to send you into the fight, but you must be properly equipped: *"And how are they to preach unless they are sent? As it is written, 'How beautiful are the feet of those who preach the good news!'"* (Romans 10:5). Satan would love to keep you on the sidelines, so put your **Gospel of Peace** shoes on!

We also are instructed to take up the **Shield of Faith.** Doubt is a primary weapon of the devil. His arrows of doubt come in many forms. Some come through the teachings of skeptical scientists, scholars, and experts who study the world, its history, and people. Satan uses the godlessness of much of academia to sow the seeds of doubt into the minds of children and students of all ages. There is nothing new about this strategy. Jesus condemned the false teachers of His day:

Woe to you, scribes and Pharisees, hypocrites! For you travel across sea and land to make a single proselyte, and when he becomes a proselyte, you make him twice as much a child of hell as yourselves.   **Matthew 23:15**

How does one become equipped with the Shield of Faith?

There is a massive body of work called *apologetics* written by Christian scholars who tackle the tough questions used by Satan to lead people away from God. An apologetic is a defense of the Christian faith.

Lee Strobel was an atheist and legal correspondent for the Chicago Tribune. He interviewed leading Christian teachers, posing the toughest questions he could muster. As each interviewee presented him with the Shield of Faith, Strobel became convinced of the Truth of the Gospel. He gave his life to Jesus Christ; the fire of his doubt was extinguished. Strobel has since written excellent apologetics books including *The Case for Faith, The Case for Christ,* and *The Case for a Creator.* There are other strong Christian apologists including Timothy Keller, Amy Orr-Ewing, Os Guinness, and Ravi Zacharias. Learn how to defend your faith by studying good apologists.

Finally, Satan wants to get into your head. He will attempt to plant seeds of insecurity in your relationship with God. **The Helmet of Salvation** is about *knowing that you know that you know* that you are indeed a child of God. Assurance comes to us as we see our lives gradually transforming as we manifest the fruit of the Holy Spirit. When we exercise the gifts of the Spirit, we experience the power of God as He uses us to minister to others. But when we get isolated from other Christians and from the nurture of the Word and Sacrament, we are vulnerable to shrink back and grow hard of hearing to the convicting Word of God. Stay close to God and draw near in full assurance of His grace. Always remember that God is a loving Father who runs to His prodigal children to keep them close to home (Luke 15). Keep your helmet on!

Besides the six pieces of defensive armor, Ephesians lists two offensive weapons for the spiritual battle: the **Sword of the Spirit** (which is the Word of God) and **Prayer**. In our congregation, we teach children how to find passages in the Bible through "sword drills." The teacher shouts out a reference and the children race to find the verse and read it. It's a fun way for children to learn their way around the Bible. Sadly, all too many adult Christians would not last long in a sword drill. The people of God are, by and large, biblically illiterate.

Perhaps that is one reason we have not seen revival in our land in so long. Great revivals in the history of Christianity are always preceded by two things: a widespread return to Bible study (both individual and in groups) and a return to the Lord in repentance and prayer. Simply put, the power of God's Holy Spirit is unleashed through the Word of God and Prayer. Listen to these words from Christian saints through the ages:

> *And Satan trembles when he sees, the weakest saint upon his knees.* —William Cowper [5]

> *The devil smiles when we make plans. He laughs when we get too busy. But he trembles when we pray—especially when we pray together. Remember, though, that it is God who answers, and He*

always answers in a way that He knows is best for everybody.
—Corrie Ten Boom [6]

The one concern of the devil is to keep Christians from praying. He fears nothing from prayerless studies, prayerless work, and prayerless religion. He laughs at our toil, mocks at our wisdom, but trembles when we pray. —Samuel Chadwick [7]

The call of the Holy Spirit is to manifest the Kingdom of God here on earth. He wants to equip the saints of God with the spiritual power and authority to fulfill that mission. So let's pray, study the Word, and put on our full armor for the battle! Then, we can truly fulfill the mission Jesus Himself gave us just before He ascended:

But you will receive power when the Holy Spirit has come upon you, and you will be my witnesses in Jerusalem and in all Judea and Samaria, and to the end of the earth.   **Acts 1:8**

WHEN WE EXERCISE THE GIFTS OF THE SPIRIT, WE EXPERIENCE THE POWER OF GOD AS HE USES US TO MINISTER TO OTHERS.

REFLECT:

Join me in this prayer: Father, we are but weak jars of clay. The things we have tried to keep in darkness, we bring to you now. Burst through any darkness, break any bondage, and take down any strongholds. Make us pure, open vessels to receive your Holy Spirit. Pour out your Spirit right now and equip us with your armor to be your witnesses in power to the ends of the earth! Amen.

_____

_____

_____

_____

_____

_____

_____

_____

_____

_____

ANOINTED: THE MISSION OF THE SPIRIT

BUT YOU ARE A CHOSEN RACE, A ROYAL PRIEST-
HOOD, A HOLY NATION, A PEOPLE FOR HIS OWN
POSSESSION, THAT YOU MAY PROCLAIM THE EX-
CELLENCIES OF HIM WHO CALLED YOU OUT OF
DARKNESS INTO HIS MARVELOUS LIGHT.
1 PETER 2:9

SUNDAY
DAY 36
ANOINTED ONES
READ HEBREWS 4:14-16

This week, we're going to look at what it means to be anointed by the Spirit of God.

We've covered what it means to be baptized, adopted, transformed, equipped, and empowered by the Holy Spirit. In a sense, all of these fall under the umbrella of "anointed." They are each facets of being anointed by the Holy Spirit of God.

As you may know, the Old Testament was originally written in Hebrew and the New Testament in Greek and Aramaic, all of which are translated into a single modern language in our Bibles—English. In English, the words used to describe Jesus as *Messiah*, *Christ*, and *Anointed One* all mean the same thing and are used interchangeably.

But it's helpful to look at the meaning of these words in the original languages. The Hebrew verb for "anoint" is מָשַׁח, *mashach*, which means "to smear." It was used to describe the rubbing of oil on one's skin or a piece of leather to keep it from becoming dried or cracked. That's a fairly mundane usage. However, in the Old Testament, the Israelites also used it to describe applying oil as a way of setting apart, or consecrating, special objects and people unto the Lord, such as "anointing" a king (See 1 Samuel 15:1).

The Hebrew noun מָשִׁיחַ, *messiah*, means "an anointed one." It was used to describe people in special "offices" within Israel. For example, when a priest was set apart for duty, he was marked with oil as an anointed priest of God. The term grew into a special title for one person who would come to save Israel, the Anointed One, the Messiah.

When the Hebrew Old Testament was translated into Greek (called the Septuagint), the Hebrew word *messiah* was almost always translated as the Greek word **Χριστός**, *Christos*, meaning "Anointed One." However, sometimes the Greek authors used a Greek transliteration—Μεσσία, *Messiah*—rather than *Christ*. In John 1:41, the Gospel writer makes sure his readers understand that Messiah and Christ are the same thing:

He first found his own brother Simon and said to him, "We have found the Messiah [Μεσσία]" (which means Christ [Χριστός]).

John 1:41

So whether the Scriptures are translated using the term *Anointed One, Messiah*, or *Christ*, they all mean the same thing. As one pastor quipped, "Christ is not Jesus' last name. It's a title." So when we say Jesus Christ, we could just as accurately say Jesus *Messiah* or Jesus *Anointed One*.

So what exactly does it mean that Jesus is "The Anointed One?"

Before the coming of Jesus, there were three leadership offices within Israel that were consecrated as messianic or anointed offices: the prophet, the priest, and the king. They served as mediators between God and His people.

The prophet was God's mouthpiece, calling Israel back to the covenant God made with them through Moses. Thus the prophet was considered to be of the line of Moses. The priest was anointed to mediate God's presence in the temple and administer the acts of repentance, grace, and reconciliation through the sacrificial system. All the priests of Israel were from the line of Levi. The king was considered to be of the line of David (the first faithful king of Israel). A king was anointed to administer God's rule on earth, as in heaven, by serving as governor of Israel and commander of the human armies of God.

So the prophet, priest, and king were the three messianic or anointed offices in Israel. Those who served in them were imperfect and temporary. But they foreshadowed One who would fulfill all three anointed offices for the people of God, not just for a time, but eternally! That One is Jesus. Jesus is described in the New Testament as *"a prophet mighty in deed and word before God and all the people"* (Luke 24:19). The writer of Hebrews calls him *"a great high priest"* (Hebrews 4:14). And Revelation describes Him as *"Lord of lords and King of kings"* (Revelation 17:14). Throughout the New Testament, Jesus also is called "the Son of God"—a title used to refer to the kings of Israel.

Prophet, priest, and king. This week we will explore these anointed offices and discover how we as Christians are called to live them out under the administration of Jesus. When the early Church called themselves "Christians" (Acts 11:26), they were calling themselves "the anointed ones." That is what you are! As a Spirit-filled follower of Jesus, you are anointed by God's Holy Spirit.

In our Anglican tradition, every member of the Church is not only to be baptized, but also to be anointed with oil. I recently baptized a father and son who had both surrendered their lives to Jesus. What a privilege to see two generations follow the Lord! After each of them was baptized, I made the sign of the Cross with oil on their forehead, marking them with these words, *"You are sealed by the Holy Spirit in baptism and marked as Christ's own forever"* (BCP, p. 308).

When our Bishop comes and confirms the faith of our new members, he uses the oil of chrism and also marks the person with the sign of the Cross on their forehead. This is a symbolic and sacramental act of anointing the confirmand with the Holy Spirit. The Bishop says, *"Strengthen, O Lord, your servant with your Holy Spirit; empower (name) for your service; and sustain (name) all the days of (his or her) life. Amen"* (BCP, p. 418).

The oil is the outward sign. The inward and spiritual reality is the anointing with the Holy Spirit of the new or confirmed member of the Church. All Christians are anointed by the Holy Spirit. As little "anointed ones," we are called to manifest a prophetic, priestly, and kingly role in this world under the Lordship of Jesus Christ. Our anointing in the Spirit is the power that fuels our mission!

AS A SPIRIT-FILLED
FOLLOWER OF
JESUS, YOU ARE
ANOINTED BY GOD'S
HOLY SPIRIT.

REFLECT:

Have you ever thought of yourself as being an anointed one? After reading today's devotional, what new significance does the title "Christian" have for you?

_____

_____

_____

_____

_____

_____

_____

_____

_____

_____

PROPHETS: HEAR THE WORD OF THE LORD
READ 2 PETER 1:19-21

Moses had a huge job in leading the people of Israel out of Egypt. They were never satisfied!

They constantly complained about Moses' leadership and the Lord's provisions of water, bread, and meat. On one occasion, Moses lamented to the Lord, *"I am not able to carry all this people alone; the burden is too heavy for me"* (Numbers 11:14).

The Lord's solution was to appoint seventy elders to share the load of prophesying God's word:

And [Moses] gathered seventy men of the elders of the people and placed them around the tent. Then the Lord came down in the cloud and spoke to him, and took some of the Spirit that was on him and put it on the seventy elders. And as soon as the Spirit rested on them, they prophesied.   **Numbers 11:24-25**

Reflecting back on the ministry of prophets through redemptive history, Peter writes, *"For no prophecy was ever produced by the will of man, but men spoke from God as they were carried along by the Holy Spirit"* (2 Peter 1:21). A prophet is a Spirit-anointed spokesperson for God. They serve as ambassadors of God's word and will to His people.

Moses was the first prophet. The instructions given from God through Moses were recorded in the Torah, the first five books of the Bible. The Torah functioned as the legal constitution of ancient Israel, often called the Law of Moses. The prophets of Israel who followed built on this foundation by calling the people of God back to faithfulness to the Lord's covenant through Moses.

The spiritual gift of prophecy has been a tremendous blessing to humanity. God, the Creator of mankind, has not left His people to wonder and wander without guidance or instruction. Through the prophet's words, people can know God's will, hear encouragement for their faithfulness, and receive rebuke and warning for their waywardness.

However, not all people have valued or remained attentive to the prophetic word. Some have taken the Word of God for granted, lost focus on it, and grown hard-hearted to it, like Israel often did. Many do not appreciate being called to account; for this reason, prophets were often ignored and even persecuted.

Long ago, at many times and in many ways, God spoke to our fathers by the prophets, but in these last days he has spoken to us by his Son, whom he appointed the heir of all things, through whom also he created the world.   **Hebrews 1:1-2**

As Jesus began His ministry, following His anointing by the Holy Spirit in baptism, He was widely recognized as *"a prophet mighty in deed and word"* (Luke 24:19). In fact, it was Jesus' prophetic ministry for which He was most well known. When Jesus asked His disciples, *"Who do people say that I am?"* They answered, *"John the Baptist; and others say, Elijah; and others, one of the prophets"* (Mark 8:27-28).

Following a miraculous healing of a lame beggar in the Temple, Peter addressed the crowd and announced that Jesus was the fulfillment of Moses' prophecy of a coming prophet:

Repent therefore, and turn back, that your sins may be blotted out, that times of refreshing may come from the presence of the Lord, and that he may send the Christ appointed for you, Jesus, whom heaven must receive until the time for restoring all the things about which God spoke by the mouth of his holy prophets long ago. Moses said, "The Lord God will raise up for you a prophet like me from your brothers. You shall listen to him in whatever he tells you..."

Acts 3:19-22

Jesus is the Great Prophet who was long awaited! Moses was considered to be a prophet like no other because he was able to enter the Tent of Meeting with God and *"speak mouth to mouth, clearly, and not in riddles"* (Numbers 12:8). Joshua memorialized Moses: *"And there has not arisen a prophet since in Israel like Moses, whom the Lord knew face to face, none like him for all the signs and the wonders that the Lord sent him to do..."* (Deuteronomy 34:10-11).

But with the coming of Jesus, Moses' prophetic office has been surpassed. That's because Jesus not only spoke the prophetic word, but also incarnated it (gave it flesh) in His very person. The Son of God is the supreme and ultimate revelation of God's will and word to the world.

The Gospel writer John puts it this way: *"The Word became flesh and made his dwelling among us"* (John 1:14, NIV). The literal meaning is that He pitched His tent among us. Moses went into the Tent of Meeting to see the glory of God. Jesus IS the tent of meeting in which all the fullness of the glory of God dwells!

John continues:

No one has ever seen God, but the one and only Son, who is himself God and is in closest relationship with the Father, has made him known.

John 1:18 (NIV)

The Word therefore no longer needs to be mediated through earthly prophets. Anyone who speaks directly with Jesus is having the same interchange that Moses experienced in the Tent of Meeting. To know Jesus is to know the Lord face to face. Jesus is the supreme prophetic Word of God.

In my relationship with God, I have had to learn how to listen to the voice of Jesus as He speaks to me through the indwelling Holy Spirit. God reveals Himself. Our intimacy with Jesus is key to hearing it. When I am not spending time in solitary prayer and devotional reading of the Scriptures, I have a more difficult time hearing Jesus' prophetic word. But when I can quiet my mind and heart in His presence and seek His face, a flood of light and revelation is often released into my heart and mind. The Lord's wisdom has recognizable characteristics. James says, *"But the wisdom from above is first pure, then peaceable, gentle, open to reason, full of mercy and good fruits, impartial and sincere"* (James 3:17). When I discern this fruit, I trust that it is the Lord's wisdom being revealed, and I obey.

GOD REVEALS HIMSELF. OUR INTIMACY WITH JESUS IS KEY TO HEARING IT.

As a Spirit-filled Christian, God has placed the very glory of Jesus Christ in you. You are a Tent of Meeting where the glory of Jesus' transfigured face shines: *"For God, who said, 'Let light shine out of darkness,' has shone in our hearts to give the light of the knowledge of the glory of God in the face of Jesus Christ"* (2 Corinthians 4:6). Meet with Him in the tent. Hear His prophetic word, and let His light shine through you!

REFLECT:

Jesus was the Great Prophet because He didn't just speak the Word of God; He *was* the Word of God among us and now in us. How do you personally discern the voice of Jesus speaking to you and revealing His will? What do you sense that the Lord is saying to you today, and how are you to respond to that voice? Draw near to Him!

_____

_____

_____

_____

_____

_____

_____

_____

_____

_____

_____

TUESDAY
DAY 38
THE WORD MADE FLESH
READ NUMBERS 11:24-30

When we are anointed with the Spirit of Christ, the Word of God is literally being written on our hearts.

Moses received the Word of God written on tablets of stone. But the New Covenant is written on tablets of flesh, our hearts:

'The days are coming,' declares the LORD, 'when I will make a new covenant with the people of Israel and with the people of Judah.... This is the covenant I will make with the people of Israel after that time,' declares the LORD. 'I will put my law in their minds and write it on their hearts.' **Jeremiah 31:31-33 (NIV)**

And the Prophet Ezekiel confirms this:

I will give you a new heart and put a new spirit in you; I will remove from you your heart of stone and give you a heart of flesh. And I will put my Spirit in you and move you to follow my decrees and be careful to keep my laws. **Ezekiel 36:26-27 (NIV)**

When Moses came out of the Tent of Meeting after convening with God, his face shone with reflected glory. It was so bright he had to put a veil over it! But the glory that shines in and through us is not reflected glory, but something greater:

For what was glorious has no glory now in comparison with the surpassing glory. And if what was transitory came with glory, how much greater is the glory of that which lasts!

2 Corinthians 3:10-11 (NIV)

Permanent glory! By the anointing of the Spirit, we have been given the glory of that which lasts. The light of Jesus Christ is shining from within us—internal glory—that we might be prophetic witnesses to Jesus, not only with our words, but also by our very lives. Paul writes that we should *"act with great boldness"* (2 Corinthians 3:12) because our lives reflect Christ. He goes on:

And we all, with unveiled face, beholding the glory of the Lord, are being transformed into the same image from one degree of glory to another. For this comes from the Lord who is the Spirit.

2 Corinthians 3:18

As we gaze into the face of Jesus, the Scriptures declare that we become transfigured from one degree of glory to another.

You are the light of the world. Do not cover your brightness! Allow your life to shine before men. Our lives are literally to become an open book that tells the story of Jesus, to be read by all. We are to live in witness to Jesus, with integrity in what we say and how we live, so that *"by the open statement of the truth we would commend ourselves to everyone's conscience in the sight of God"* (2 Corinthians 4:2).

I was asked by Michael to pray for him, that he would speak boldly and become more authentic and vulnerable in expressing his faith with some unbelieving co-workers. They were harming the company by their unethical and corrupt behavior. Through encouragement and seeking boldness from God, Michael gained confidence to stand in the face of those who would silence his witness in the workplace.

It is hard to be a light, especially with those closest to you, such as family, friends, and co-workers. But beloved, that is your calling. Understand that people have always sought to intimidate and shame prophets into silence. They will do the same with you.

You are anointed to be a prophet of God. The plan has always been that God would make all of His people prophets. As Moses was appointing the seventy elders to assist him, two of the first prophets, Eldad and Medad, were prophesying to the people of God inside the camp. Joshua was concerned about preserving the authority of Moses as God's anointed spokesperson:

And Joshua the son of Nun, the assistant of Moses from his youth, said, "My lord Moses, stop them." But Moses said to him, "Are you jealous for my sake? Would that all the Lord's people were prophets, that the Lord would put his Spirit on them!" And Moses and the elders of Israel returned to the camp.   **Numbers 11:28-30**

Moses may not have realized it, but he was actually vocalizing the larger plan of God. Indeed, all of God's people would be anointed prophets following the coming of the Anointed One. Through the prophet Joel, God announced that the Holy Spirit would be poured out on all people:

And it shall come to pass afterward, that I will pour out my Spirit on all flesh; your sons and your daughters shall prophesy, your old men shall dream dreams, and your young men shall see visions. Even on the male and female servants in those days I will pour out my Spirit.   **Joel 2:28-29**

We are living in a time of prophetic anointing. A prophet of God spoke the good news of Jesus to you, and you called on the name of the Lord and were saved. God is raising up an army of prophets to share the announcement of the Good News of Jesus to a lost world. He is calling all people on this planet to the *"obedience of faith"* (Romans 1:5) through His prophets. That means you!

REFLECT:

Who was the person who spoke the Good News of Jesus to you?
Have you ever thought of this person as a *prophet*? You, too, are
a prophet, anointed in the Spirit to be a voice for His reconciling
love, His absolute truth, and His peace and justice. Are others see-
ing the living example of Christ in you? Ask God to help you fully
live your prophetic role today.

_____

_____

_____

_____

_____

_____

_____

_____

_____

_____

PRIESTS: DRAW NEAR TO THE THRONE OF GRACE

READ HEBREWS 10:11-14

Yesterday we looked at the first anointed office of *prophet*. Today we'll take a look at the second anointed office under the Old Covenant, the *priesthood*.

The primary role of the priest in Israel was to offer sacrifices in the Temple on behalf of the people. Essentially, priests served as mediators of God's grace and truth. They taught the people how to live holy lives before the Lord. And when the people of God sinned, they would make substitutionary atonement—the life of a lamb without blemish for the life of the sinner. *"Indeed, under the law almost everything is purified with blood, and without the shedding of blood there is no forgiveness of sins"* (Hebrews 9:22).

The priests of Israel were anointed: *"[Moses] poured some of the anointing oil on Aaron's head and anointed him to consecrate him"* (Leviticus 8:12). Jesus, too, was anointed as a high priest, in His baptism. God the Father anointed Jesus with the Holy Spirit and the divine voice of commissioning: *"This is my beloved Son, with whom I am well pleased"* (Matthew 3:17). The writer of Hebrews reiterates Jesus' anointing: *"So also Christ did not exalt himself to*

*be made a high priest, but was ap-
pointed by him who said to him,
'You are my Son...'"* (Hebrews 5:5).

Like the priests of Israel, Jesus also
would make atonement for sins
through a sacrifice. Only, in His
case, Jesus himself would become
the sacrifice, making atonement
for sin, once and for all, through
His death on the Cross for the
whole world!

Jesus, then, was both priest and
victim, and His sacrifice was far
above that of animals, as the writer of Hebrews explains:

*For if the blood of goats and bulls,
and the sprinkling of defiled persons with the ashes of a heifer,
sanctify for the purification of
the flesh, how much more will
the blood of Christ, who through
the eternal Spirit offered himself
without blemish to God, purify
our conscience from dead works to
serve the living God.*
Hebrews 9:13-14

In the old days, the high priest
had to make continual sacrifices
for his own sins and the sins of
the people. He never rested from
his duties because people never
rested from their sin. The blood of

JESUS CHANGED EVERYTHING! HIS SACRIFICE FOR SIN WAS SUPREME, ONCE AND FOR ALL.

bulls and goats was required for every new sin because it wasn't a real, eternal payment for sin (See Hebrews 10:4). The altars of Israel had a continual flow of the blood of sacrificed animals. That may sound disgusting, but that is the disgusting nature of the problem of sin: it never stops. It continues to flow from our hearts and destroys our intimacy with God and others.

But Jesus changed everything! His sacrifice for sin was supreme, once and for all. It wasn't a temporary fix; it was eternal redemption for all sins—past, present, and future—for those who would accept His sacrifice on their behalf.

When you make a purchase with a credit card, you get to take home the purchased item. But that item isn't truly paid for until the money is transferred and the payment is made. In the same way, the Old Testament sacrifice of bulls and goats allowed sinners to "take home" forgiveness, but the true payment for their sin wasn't made until Christ's death on the Cross. That was the cosmic transaction of the only perfect One who ever lived sacrificing His life for us—a payment for sin, eternal, for all.

Now there is no longer any offering of sin needed—ever again! If you have given your life to Jesus and been anointed by His Spirit, you have been forgiven and justice has been satisfied once and for all. Every sin that you have committed, every sin you ever will commit, has been forgiven—forever.

After His Resurrection, Jesus entered into the true temple in the heavenly realms, and sat at the right hand of God:

But when Christ had offered for all time a single sacrifice for sins, he sat down at the right hand of God, waiting from that time until his enemies should be made a footstool for his feet. For by a single offering he has perfected for all time those who are being sanctified.
Hebrews 10:12-14

The practical application is that every believer can walk right into the presence of a Holy, Holy, Holy God without guilt or shame, or fear of punishment or condemnation. Such knowledge is awesome, humbling, and beautiful. Jesus has justified you and me, both now and forever.

How long have you borne the shame and embarrassment of the evils you have done, spoken, or thought? By the anointing Holy Spirit of your Great High Priest, your conscience is being purified and your defilements washed away. Only, there is something essential that you must do.

Draw near.

Draw near to Him. Our shame and guilt, our feelings of unworthiness, our struggles against temptations in the flesh, our hurts and pains, and even our fear of the pain of healing can cause us to harden our hearts to the voice of the Great High Priest—to shrink back.

Once, a child had fallen prey to pornographic videos on the Internet. When his parents discovered it, he felt dirty, exposed, and ashamed. Those are the feelings of sin. When his mother went to talk with him, the young boy was nowhere to be found. He had run away and hidden himself. She searched and found him outside in the backyard in a hole he had dug, covered with dirt.

The boy's parents brought him home, cleaned him up, and washed him with water. They also shared the grace and forgiveness of Jesus Christ. His father said, "Son, Jesus died for that sin and all of your others. He knows you and loves you and paid the price to forgive you. He is not mad at you, and neither am I."

What a blessing to hear the Gospel of the Great High Priest and Savior when you need it most! In your darkest moments, you may be tempted to find a hole and cover yourself with dirt. Do not shrink back! Instead, draw near to the Throne of Grace.

Since we have a great priest over the house of God, let us draw near with a true heart in full assurance of faith, with our hearts sprinkled clean from an evil conscience and our bodies washed with pure water. Let us hold fast the confession of our hope without wavering, for he who promised is faithful.   **Hebrews 10:21-23**

He who promised *IS* faithful. His name is Jesus. Draw near to Him.

REFLECT:

When have you experienced overwhelming guilt or shame because of a sin you committed or sin that was committed against
you? What did you do? If you are still carrying that burden, take it
to the Throne of Grace right now. Draw near to Jesus. He is your
High Priest. Let Him wash your body with pure water and sprinkle
your heart and conscience clean. He is waiting for you. Go now!

_____

_____

_____

_____

_____

_____

_____

_____

_____

_____

THURSDAY
DAY 40
THE PRIESTHOOD OF ALL BELIEVERS
READ ISAIAH 6:1-8

In the Old Testament, there was a special class of people anointed as priests. However, the entire nation of Israel was to see itself in a priestly role:

Now therefore, if you will indeed obey my voice and keep my covenant, you shall be my treasured possession among all peoples, for all the earth is mine; and you shall be to me a kingdom of priests and a holy nation.   **Exodus 19:5-6**

The people of Israel had a very special role to play for the other nations. They knew the one true God and Creator of humankind! Therefore, each and every Israelite was to serve as an ambassador, a priest, announcing God's rule and grace to the rest of the world. A kingdom of priests. God promised that through the descendants of Abraham all the nations of the world would be blessed.

In the Old Testament, the Temple was the center of Israelite worship. However, in the Temple courtyard was a section where people from other nations could gather to worship the Lord as well. It was fittingly called the Court of the Nations. Here, like a priest, Israel mediated God's presence to others, inviting all people to come and find forgiveness for sins and reconciliation with the one true God of Israel.

As Christians, we are anointed with the Holy Spirit by the great High Priest, Jesus. As such, we become part of the royal priesthood of God. The apostle Peter writes:

As you come to him, a living stone rejected by men but in the sight of God chosen and precious, you yourselves like living stones are being built up as a spiritual house, to be a holy priesthood...   **1 Peter 2:4-5**

So what exactly does a holy priesthood do? The primary job of a priest is to serve in the ministry of reconciliation, helping people be reconciled to God through Jesus Christ. Therefore, through our life and witness, God is reconciling the world to himself. As Paul writes:

All this is from God, who through Christ reconciled us to himself and gave us the ministry of reconciliation; that is, in Christ God was reconciling the world to himself, not counting their trespasses against them, and entrusting to us the message of reconciliation. Therefore, we are ambassadors for Christ, God making his appeal through us.
                                          2 Corinthians 5:18-20a

At the beginning of my junior year at the University of Florida, while attending a class on advertising, I noticed a friend I had not seen since high school. His name was Bartow McDonald. As we walked out of class, Bartow and I reconnected. Each day afterward, he would share what the Lord was doing in his life. Eventually, Bartow invited me to a Bible Study and encouraged me to be reconciled to God through Jesus.

I was spiritually lost at the time; I was without God and had very little direction or hope. The Lord anointed Bartow to be the one to speak to me and invite me to draw near to Jesus. Through his vulnerability and gracious attitude, I was able to hear the good news that God wanted to be in a personal relationship with me and respond in faith and trust. Bartow served as a royal priest to me.

Can you remember the people in your life who served as mediators of God's reconciling love and forgiveness to you? Who were they? What did they say? How did these chosen ones convey God's grace to you? All Christians are called to lead others to the throne room of grace—into the presence of Jesus.

As we have been forgiven, so we are now called to be ambassadors of God's forgiveness and grace. The Court of Nations is all around us. And the New Temple is us, the Church!

The key to being an effective ambassador is to find your confidence in the anointing of the Holy Spirit. None of us has any power in and of ourselves to reconcile another person to God. But God makes His appeal through us. We must simply allow Him to use our lips and lives.

While visiting the Temple of the Old Testament, a man named Isaiah was caught up into the throne room of heaven in a vision. There he saw the Lord on His throne *"high and lifted up; and the train of his robe filled the temple"* (Isaiah 6:1). The Lord called Isaiah to become a spokesperson for Him. Yet Isaiah felt unworthy to the task. In fact, in the presence of God's holiness, he despaired of his very life: *"Woe is me! For I am lost; for I am a man of unclean lips, and I dwell in the midst of a people of unclean lips"* (Isaiah 6:5).

So the Lord appointed a coal to be taken from the heavenly altar to purify Isaiah's lips, saying, *"Behold, this has touched your lips; your guilt is taken away, and your sin atoned for"* (Isaiah 6:6). Jesus, our Great High Priest, has purified us and made us a holy priesthood to serve as His messengers.

The Lord asked Isaiah, *"Whom shall I send?"* Today, He is asking the same of you and me. Our response is to be one of willing surrender, as Isaiah's was: *"Here I am, Lord. Send me!"* (Isaiah 6:8).

Our strength is not in ourselves, but in the reconciling power of Jesus and the inner workings of the Holy Spirit. Our lives are to be living sacrifices. Jesus uses whatever we sacrifice to Him for His Glory and good will. Offer Him your hands and feet, and He will use you to serve and bless others. Offer Him your money, and He will make you a conduit of generosity to build up the Kingdom. Allow Him to open your mouth, and you will become a priestly ambassador of grace!

REFLECT:

If you are an anointed child of God through faith in Jesus, you are a priest! How does that make you feel? If unworthy, you are in good company. We are all unworthy of the call, yet God graciously cleanses and purifies us so that we may be His ambassadors. As a priest, how can you speak, give, or serve this week in a way that will help reconcile the world to its Creator?

_____

_____

_____

_____

_____

_____

_____

_____

_____

_____

_____

FRIDAY
DAY 41
KINGS: CONFESS THAT JESUS CHRIST IS LORD
READ JOHN 13:1-17

Bob Dylan had it right, "You gotta serve somebody!" Left to our own direction and devices, we wander and stray *"like sheep without a shepherd"* (1 Kings 22:17, Matthew 9:36).

In the Old Testament, the people of Israel were ruled for a time by judges. They cycled through a familiar pattern of falling away from God, enduring the consequences, crying out to God for deliverance, and God delivering them. But each time, they fell away from God again. In the concluding words of the book of Judges, everyone *"did what is right in his own eyes"* (Judges 21:25).

Israel recognized that it needed a king; but they cried out for a human king *"like other nations"* (1 Samuel 8:5). Jesus would teach that the rulers of the nations of this world are not to be desired—they are tyrants who use authority and power to *"lord it over"* their subjects (Mark 10:42).

In our day, we see far too many examples of poor leadership on the part of human rulers who seek their own political interests over the common good. God is the only truly benevolent, gracious, and right Ruler of the people of this world. He has appointed His King—Jesus, the Son of God!

Since Israel demanded a human king, God Himself appointed that king—one who would seek the Lord first in his decisions and aim to do right in the sight of the Lord. The prophet Samuel anointed David as king:

And the Lord said, "Arise, anoint him, for this is he." Then Samuel took the horn of oil and anointed him in the midst of his brothers. And the Spirit of the Lord rushed upon David from that day forward.   **1 Samuel 16:12-13**

Interestingly, the kings of Israel enjoyed another title: Son of God. When the reign of a new king was inaugurated, the leaders used the liturgy of Psalm 2 in which the Lord says to the Anointed One, *"You are my son, today I have begotten you!"* (Psalm 2:7). The complete fulfillment of this prophecy would come with the reign of King Jesus.

The Scriptures declare that Jesus' right to rule is grounded in His loving sacrifice as a Good Shepherd who laid down His life for His sheep. Jesus said, *"...the Son of Man came not to be served but to serve and to give his life as a ransom for many"* (Matthew 20:28). The character of Jesus' kingly rule is one of self-sacrifice and humility. Where do we see such servant-leadership in the worldly presidents, rulers, dictators, and kings of our age?

And being found in human form, he humbled himself by becoming obedient to the point of death, even death on a cross. Therefore God has highly exalted him and bestowed on him the name that is above every name, so that at the name of Jesus every knee should bow, in heaven and on earth and under the earth, and every tongue confess that Jesus Christ is Lord, to the glory of God the Father.

Philippians 2:8-11

Jesus wins the world to Himself by being lifted up on a Cross of shame rather than an earthly throne of power.

Our anointing by the Spirit is to come under Jesus' kingly rule of service and grace. The Apostle Peter learned what it means to submit to Jesus' gracious shepherding. As Jesus prepared His disciples for His coming death, He bent down to wash Peter's feet. This was a servant's task! Peter could not accept such a humiliating gesture from his King: *"'You shall never wash my feet,' Peter declared. Jesus answered him, 'If I do not wash you, you have no share with me'"* (John 13:8).

In our pride, it is hard to receive service from those above us. Can you imagine the President of the United States, the Pope, or the Queen of England stooping down to wash your feet? Would you let them do so if they tried? Would such a leader even offer? Consider that the Lord of the Universe, the King of Heaven and Earth Himself, has stooped low to wash not just your feet, but your soul as well.

When Jesus said to Peter, *"If I do not wash you, you have no share with me,"* He was saying that without humbling ourselves to accept Jesus as our serving Savior, we cannot have Him as our King. We need to humbly subject ourselves to His humility. We must bend our heads low to come under the service of a servant king. The plan of God is that all Creation in heaven and on earth would humble itself and be brought together under Jesus' most gracious rule.

So what is our role in bringing the Kingdom of God to earth *"as it is in heaven"* (Matthew 6:10)? Just as Jesus anoints us to be prophets and priests, He also anoints us to be kings—priestly kings who represent Jesus' rule on Earth. Amazingly, the Scriptures declare that we are already seated with Jesus as vice-regents and co-rulers:

And God raised us up with Christ and seated us with him in the heavenly realms in Christ Jesus, in order that in the coming ages he might show the incomparable riches of his grace...

Ephesians 2:6-7

How do we manifest Jesus' rule on Earth? The key is to do so as Jesus did, with grace and humility. The world is won to Christ not by an exercise of worldly strength and intimidation, but by the administration of self-sacrificial service and love. That does not mean that Christians are weak rulers. Quite the contrary! With respect to fighting against spiritual forces and authorities, we are called to wage war without mercy, using every spiritual weapon at our disposal. But when it comes to human souls, we are to woo them to the rule of Jesus by stooping low to wash their feet. As both mighty warriors and humble servants, the "gates of hell" will not prevail against us!

As kingly ambassadors of the Lord, the Great Commission is our primary mission. That mission is an outworking of Jesus' ascension as King of Heaven and Earth. And our authority to fulfill this mission is the very authority of Jesus:

All authority in heaven and on earth has been given to me. Therefore go and make disciples of all nations, baptizing them in the name of the Father and of the Son and of the Holy Spirit, and teaching them to obey everything I have commanded you. And surely I am with you always, to the very end of the age.   **Matthew 28:18-20**

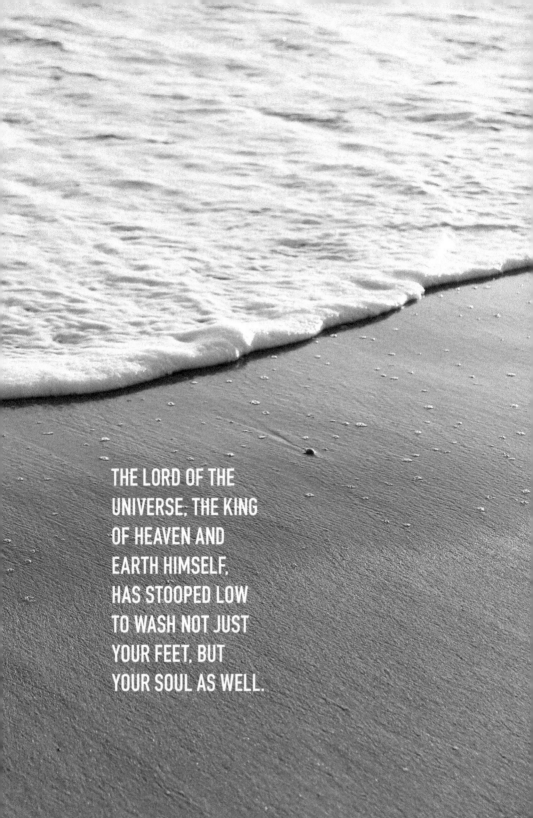

THE LORD OF THE
UNIVERSE, THE KING
OF HEAVEN AND
EARTH HIMSELF,
HAS STOOPED LOW
TO WASH NOT JUST
YOUR FEET, BUT
YOUR SOUL AS WELL.

REFLECT:

Do you see yourself on an anointed mission from God? Your royal marching orders are to go and make disciples of all nations, baptizing them into the Christian life and teaching them to follow Jesus. The good news is, you are not alone in the fulfillment of your kingly call. Jesus promises that, thorough His anointing Spirit, He will be with you always, to the very end of the age!

_____

_____

_____

_____

_____

_____

_____

_____

_____

_____

_____

DAY 42
SATURDAY
THE SPIRIT OF THE LORD HAS ANOINTED ME!
READ ISAIAH 61:1-11

One of the more powerful scenes in the New Testament is when Jesus is attending worship at a gathering in Nazareth. All eyes are upon Him as He unrolls a scroll of the prophet Isaiah and quotes from this passage:

The Spirit of the Lord God is upon me, because the Lord has anointed me to bring good news to the poor; he has sent me to bind up the brokenhearted, to proclaim liberty to the captives, and the opening of the prison to those who are bound; to proclaim the year of the Lord's favor, and the day of vengeance of our God; to comfort all who mourn; to grant to those who mourn in Zion—to give them a beautiful headdress instead of ashes, the oil of gladness instead of mourning, the garment of praise instead of a faint spirit; that they may be called oaks of righteousness, the planting of the Lord, that he may be glorified. **Isaiah 61:1-3**

The Jews listening to Jesus would have been familiar with this prophetic passage—a passage that pointed to a coming Messiah.

What startled them was what happened when Jesus closed the scroll. He turned to them and said, *"Today this scripture is fulfilled in your hearing"* (Luke 4:21).

Jesus was declaring that He was, and is, the Messiah! He was, and is, the one who binds up your broken heart, comforts you in your grief, and strengthens you for life as an *"oak of righteousness."*

The Anointed One alone brings restoration and reversal of fortunes to the people of God. He promises to overthrow oppressors and bring about renewal and restoration in your life. Jesus accomplishes this through the powerful work of the Holy Spirit.

But these purposes have a greater end than just personal restoration for those who are the recipients of the Spirit's anointing. We who are anointed are anointed to be a blessing to others. Let's keep reading Isaiah 61:

They shall build up the ancient ruins; they shall raise up the former devastations; they shall repair the ruined cities, the devastations of many generations.   **Isaiah 61:4**

Those who have been rebuilt, restored, and renewed will then become rebuilders, restorers, and renewers. Do you see it? The Anointed One's ministry will be multiplied through the people whom He blesses. You will rebuild, restore, and renew. This is the fulfillment of the promises to Abraham that, *"all peoples on earth will be blessed through you"* (Genesis 12:3, NIV). We are blessed by the King to be a blessing to the people of the world. The purpose of God is the renewal of righteousness upon the entire face of the earth!

I will greatly rejoice in the Lord; my soul shall exult in my God, for he has clothed me with the garments of salvation; he has covered me with the robe of righteousness, as a bridegroom decks himself like a priest with a beautiful headdress, and as a bride adorns herself with her jewels. For as the earth brings forth its sprouts, and as a garden causes what is sown in it to sprout up, so the Lord God will cause righteousness and praise to sprout up before all the nations.
                                                    Isaiah 61:10-11

The ultimate purpose of the Anointed One is to renew the face of the earth as a garden of righteousness and praise. The vision of the Anointed One prophesied in the Old Testament is that He would heal and restore the hurting and broken so that they could go out and heal and restore the entire planet.

Our job is to bring about the reign of God on earth as it is in heaven. We do not do this with earthly power or authority, but by the Word proclaimed and the wind and breath of the Spirit of God enlivening us.

So, look around. Open your eyes. What do you see in the world around you? Has the benevolent rule of the Anointed One manifested? Or are the people around you still harassed and helpless, like sheep without a shepherd?

Our Great Commission is grounded in the authority of the King. Jesus sends out His people in the authority of His anointing presence and the Holy Spirit:

And Jesus came and said to them, "All authority in heaven and on earth has been given to me. Go therefore and make disciples of all nations, baptizing them in the name of the Father and of the Son and of the Holy Spirit, teaching them to observe all that I have commanded you. And behold, I am with you always, to the end of the age." **Matthew 28:18-20**

As Christians, our primary job is to bring people into the Spirit-filled Life as disciples of Jesus. We are all called to invite others to come under the Kingdom of God by first being baptized in the name of the Father, Son, and Holy Spirit. And then, after people are baptized by water, anointed by the Holy Spirit, and marked as Christ's own forever, our next task is to teach them how to submit their lives to the King by observing all that He has commanded.

The Spirit of the Lord is upon you. He has anointed you to proclaim the good news to the poor, to bind up the brokenhearted, to announce liberty to those held captive by spiritual and earthly oppressions.

The power of God is coursing through your very being to rebuild, restore, and renew. Become a servant of the Servant King, Jesus, and may the garden of God's hope and righteousness sprout up in your life and before all the nations of this world.

This is what it means to live the Spirit-filled Life. It is an adventure like no other!

AS CHRISTIANS, OUR PRIMARY JOB IS TO BRING PEOPLE INTO THE SPIRIT-FILLED LIFE AS DISCIPLES OF JESUS.

REFLECT:

How does it make you feel to know that the power of God's Spirit is coursing through you to rebuild, restore, and renew the earth? Does it seem an overwhelming task? Remember, it is the Holy Spirit who is at work, in you and through you. You just need to be a willing vessel. Tell your Heavenly Father you are willing today. Begin the adventure of a truly Spirit-filled Life!

_____

_____

_____

_____

_____

_____

_____

_____

_____

_____

_____

END NOTES

Week One: Baptized

(Page 39) [1] C.S. Lewis, *Mere Christianity*, (New York: Macmillan, 1960), 38-39.

(Page 40) [2] Bishop John W. Howe, *Anointed by the Spirit: A Study of the Ministry of Jesus and His Followers*, (Lake Mary, FL: Creation House, 2012), 15.

Week Two: Adopted

(Page 68) [1] Jen Hatmaker, "The Truth About Adoption: One Year Later," Jen Hatmaker Blog, [web blog], 21 August 2012, http://jenhatmaker.com/blog/2012/08/21/the-truth-about-adoption-one-year-later.

Week Three: Transformed

(Page 88) [1] C.S. Lewis, *The Great Divorce*, (New York: Macmillian Publishing Company, 1946), 98-105.

(Page 91) [2] A.W. Tozer, Man: *The Dwelling Place of God*, (Camp Hill: Christian Publications, 1966), 46-47.

(Page 107) [3] Henry Drummond, *The Greatest Thing in the World*, (London: Hodder and Stoughton, 1890), 31.

(Page 108) [4] Ibid., 20-21.

(Page 109) [5] Ibid., 21.

Week Four: Equipped

(Page 146) [1] *Chariots of Fire*, dir. Hugh Hudson, USA, Twentieth Century-Fox, 1981, [videocassette].

Week 5: Empowered

(Page 172) [1] Henri Nouwen, The Wounded Healer, (New York: Image Books, 1979).

(Page 176) [2] These three Gospels are called "synoptic" because they are all written with a similar literary structure and basic outline though with important differences. John's Gospel follows an entirely different literary structure.

(Page 179) [3] Charles Spurgeon, *Christ's Words from the Cross*, (Grand Rapids: Baker Books, 1986), 24-25.

(Page 180) [4] Edward Perronet, *All Hail the Power of Jesus' Name*, 1779, The Hymnal 1982, (New York: The Church Hymnal Corporation, 1986), numbers 450 & 451.

(Page 196) [5] William Cowper, *What Various Hindrances We Meet*, 1779, Olney Hymns, (London: W. Oliver, 1779), number 60.

(Page 197) [6] Corrie Ten Boom, *Jesus is Victor*, (Kingsway Publications Ltd., 1985).

(Page 197) [7] Samuel Chadwick, https://en.wikipedia.org/wiki/Samuel_Chadwick, 1860-1932, (accessed July 2015).

ARTWORK ATTRIBUTION

Page 5 – The Pentecost (oil on canvas), Galloche, Louis (1670-1761) / Musee des Beaux-Arts, Nantes, France / Bridgeman Images.

Page 41 – The Baptism of Christ, c.1597 (oil on canvas), Greco, El (Domenico Theotocopuli) (1541-1614) / Prado, Madrid, Spain / Peter Willi / Bridgeman Images.

Page 45 – Ms Lat. Q.v.l. 126 f.90 The Holy Spirit, from the 'Book of Hours of Louis d'Orleans', 1469 (vellum), Colombe, Jean (c.1430-c.1493) / National Library, St. Petersburg, Russia / Bridgeman Images.

Page 60 – Vision of St. John of Matha, by Giovanni Antonio Guardi, 18th Century (canvas), Guardi, Giovanni Antonio (1698-1760) / Mondadori Portfolio/Electa/Elio Ciol / Bridgeman Images.

Page 77 – The Transfiguration, 1594-95 (oil on canvas), Carracci, Lodovico (1555-1619) / Pinacoteca Nazionale, Bologna, Italy / Bridgeman Images.

Page 113 – St. Francis Xavier Blessing the Sick (oil on canvas), Rubens, Peter Paul (1577-1640) / Kunsthistorisches Museum, Vienna, Austria / Bridgeman Images.

Page 157 – Archangel Michael Defeating Satan, c.1636 (oil on canvas), Reni, Guido (1575-1642) / Santa Maria della Concezione, Rome, Italy / Bridgeman Images.

Page 177 – The Heavenly Militia, c.1348-54 (tempera on panel), Guariento, Ridolfo di Arpo (c.1310-c.1370) / Museo Civico, Padua, Italy / Bridgeman Images.

Page 201 – The Entry of Christ into Jerusalem (oil on panel), Santi di Tito (1536-1603) / Galleria dell' Accademia, Florence, Italy / Bridgeman Images.

NOTES